MACINTOSH SYSTEM 7.5 FOR DUMMIES™

Quick Reference

by Stuart J. Stuple

IDG BOOKS

IDG Books Worldwide, Inc.
An International Data Group Company

Foster City, CA ♦ Chicago, IL ♦ Indianapolis, IN ♦ Braintree, MA ♦ Dallas, TX

Macintosh System 7.5 For Dummies™ Quick Reference

Published by
IDG Books Worldwide, Inc.
An International Data Group Company
919 E. Hillsdale Blvd.
Suite 400
Foster City, CA 94404

Library of Congress Catalog Card No.: 94-79607

ISBN: 1-56884-956-7

Printed in the United States of America

10 9 8 7 6 5 4 3 2

1A/SX/RS/ZU

Distributed in the United States by IDG Books Worldwide, Inc.

Distributed by Macmillan Canada for Canada; by Computer and Technical Books for the Caribbean Basin; by Contemporanea de Ediciones for Venezuela; by Distribuidora Cuspide for Argentina; by CITEC for Brazil; by Ediciones ZETA S.C.R. Ltda. for Peru; by Editorial Limusa SA for Mexico; by Transworld Publishers Limited in the United Kingdom and Europe; by Al-Maiman Publishers & Distributors for Saudi Arabia; by Simron Pty. Ltd. for South Africa; by IDG Communications (HK) Ltd. for Hong Kong; by Toppan Company Ltd. for Japan; by Addison Wesley Publishing Company for Korea; by Longman Singapore Publishers Ltd. for Singapore, Malaysia, Thailand and Indonesia; by Unalis Corporation for Taiwan; by WS Computer Publishing Company, Inc. for the Philippines; by WoodsLane Pty. Ltd. for Australia; by WoodsLane Enterprises Ltd. for New Zealand.

For general information on IDG Books in the U.S., including information on discounts and premiums, contact IDG Books at 800-434-3422 or 415-655-3000.

For information on where to purchase IDG Books outside the U.S., contact IDG Books International at 415-655-3021 or fax 415-655-3295.

For information on translations, contact Marc Jeffrey Mikulich, Director, Foreign & Subsidiary Rights, at IDG Books Worldwide, 415-655-3018 or fax 415-655-3295.

For sales inquiries and special prices for bulk quantities, write to the address above or call IDG Books Worldwide at 415-655-3000.

For information on using IDG Books in the classroom, or for ordering examination copies, contact Jim Kelly at 800-434-2086.

ABOUT IDG BOOKS WORLDWIDE

Welcome to the world of IDG Books Worldwide.

IDG Books Worldwide, Inc. is a subsidiary of International Data Group, the world's largest publisher of computer-related information and the leading global provider of information services on information technology. IDG was founded more than 25 years ago and now employs more than 7,000 people worldwide. IDG publishes more than 220 computer publications in 65 countries (see listing below). More than fifty million people read one or more IDG publications each month.

Launched in 1990, IDG Books Worldwide is today the #1 publisher of best-selling computer books in the United States. We are proud to have received 3 awards from the Computer Press Association in recognition of editorial excellence, and our best-selling ...*For Dummies*™ series has more than 12 million copies in print with translations in 25 languages. IDG Books, through a recent joint venture with IDG's Hi-Tech Beijing, became the first U.S. publisher to publish a computer book in the People's Republic of China. In record time, IDG Books has become the first choice for millions of readers around the world who want to learn how to better manage their businesses.

Our mission is simple: Every IDG book is designed to bring extra value and skill-building instructions to the reader. Our books are written by experts who understand and care about our readers. The knowledge base of our editorial staff comes from years of experience in publishing, education, and journalism — experience which we use to produce books for the '90s. In short, we care about books, so we attract the best people. We devote special attention to details such as audience, interior design, use of icons, and illustrations. And because we use an efficient process of authoring, editing, and desktop publishing our books electronically, we can spend more time ensuring superior content and spend less time on the technicalities of making books.

You can count on our commitment to deliver high-quality books at competitive prices on topics consumers want to read about. At IDG, we value quality, and we have been delivering quality for more than 25 years. You'll find no better book on a subject than an IDG book.

John Kilcullen
President and CEO
IDG Books Worldwide, Inc.

VIII
WINNER
Eighth Annual Computer Press Awards 1992

IX
WINNER
Ninth Annual Computer Press Awards 1993

IDG BOOKS

IDG Books Worldwide, Inc. is a subsidiary of International Data Group, the world's largest publisher of computer-related information and the leading global provider of information services on information technology. International Data Group publishes over 220 computer publications in 65 countries. More than fifty million people read one or more International Data Group publications each month. The officers are Patrick J. McGovern, Founder and Board Chairman; Kelly Conlin, President; Jim Casella, Chief Operating Officer. International Data Group's publications include: ARGENTINA'S Computerworld Argentina, Infoworld Argentina; AUSTRALIA'S Computerworld Australia, Computer Living, Australian PC World, Australian Macworld, Network World, Mobile Business Australia, Publish!, Reseller, IDG Sources; AUSTRIA'S Computerwelt Oesterreich, PC Test; BELGIUM'S Data News (CW); BOLIVIA'S Computerworld; BRAZIL'S Computerworld, Connections, Game Power, Mundo Unix, PC World, Publish, Super Game; BULGARIA'S Computerworld Bulgaria, PC & Mac World Bulgaria, Network World Bulgaria; CANADA'S CIO Canada, Computerworld Canada, InfoCanada, Network World Canada, Reseller; CHILE'S Computerworld Chile, Informatica; COLOMBIA'S Computerworld Colombia, PC World; COSTA RICA'S PC World; CZECH REPUBLIC'S Computerworld, Elektronika, PC World; DENMARK'S Communications World, Computerworld Danmark, Computerworld Focus, Macintosh Produktkatalog, Macworld Danmark, PC World Danmark, PC Produktguide, Tech World, Windows World; ECUADOR'S PC World Ecuador; EGYPT'S Computerworld (CW) Middle East, PC World Middle East; FINLAND'S MikroPC, Tietoviikko, Tietoverkko; FRANCE'S Distributique, GOLDEN MAC, InfoPC, Le Guide du Monde Informatique, Le Monde Informatique, Telecoms & Reseaux; GERMANY'S Computerwoche, Computerwoche Focus, Computerwoche Extra, Electronic Entertainment, Gamepro, Information Management, Macwelt, Netzwelt, PC Welt, Publish, Publish; GREECE'S Publish & Macworld; HONG KONG'S Computerworld Hong Kong, PC World Hong Kong; HUNGARY'S Computerworld SZT, PC World; INDIA'S Computers & Communications; INDONESIA'S Info Komputer; IRELAND'S ComputerScope; ISRAEL'S Beyond Windows, Computerworld Israel, Multimedia, PC World Israel; ITALY'S Computerworld Italia, Lotus Magazine, Macworld Italia, Networking Italia, PC Shopping Italy, PC World Italia; JAPAN'S Computerworld Today, Information Systems World, Macworld Japan, Nikkei Personal Computing, SunWorld Japan, Windows World; KENYA'S East African Computer News; KOREA'S Computerworld Korea, Macworld Korea, PC World Korea; LATIN AMERICA'S GamePro; MALAYSIA'S Computerworld Malaysia, PC World Malaysia; MEXICO'S Compu Edicion, Compu Manufactura, Computacion/Punto de Venta, Computerworld Mexico, MacWorld, Mundo Unix, PC World, Windows; THE NETHERLANDS' Computer! Totaal, Computable (CW), LAN Magazine, Lotus Magazine, MacWorld; NEW ZEALAND'S Computer Buyer, Computerworld New Zealand, Network World, New Zealand PC World; NIGERIA'S PC World Africa; NORWAY'S Computerworld Norge, Lotusworld Norge, Macworld Norge, Maxi Data, Networld, PC World Ekspress, PC World Nettverk, PC World Norge, PC World's Produktguide, Publish& Multimedia World, Student Data, Unix World, Windowsworld; PAKISTAN'S PC World Pakistan; PANAMA'S PC World Panama; PERU'S Computerworld Peru, PC World; PEOPLE'S REPUBLIC OF CHINA'S China Computerworld, China Infoworld, China PC Info Magazine, Computer Fan, PC World China, Electronics International, Electronics Today/ Multimedia World, Electronic Product World, China Network World, Software World Magazine, Telecom Product World, PHILIPPINES' Computerworld Philippines, PC Digest (PCW); POLAND'S Computerworld Poland, Computerworld Special Report, Networld, PC World/Komputer, Sunworld; PORTUGAL'S Cerebro/PC World, Correio Informatico/Computerworld, MacIn; ROMANIA'S Computerworld, PC World, Telecom Romania; RUSSIA'S Computerworld-Moscow, Mir - PK (PCW), Sety (Networks); SINGAPORE'S Computerworld Southeast Asia, PC World Singapore; SLOVENIA'S Monitor Magazine; SOUTH AFRICA'S Computer Mail (CIO),Computing S.A.,Network World S.A., Software World; SPAIN'S Advanced Systems, Amiga World, Computerworld Espana, Communicaciones World, Macworld Espana, NeXTWORLD, Super Juegos Magazine (GamePro), PC World Espana, Publish; SWEDEN'S Attack, ComputerSweden, Corporate Computing, Macworld, Mikrodatorn, Natverk & Kommunikation, PC World, CAP & Design, DataIngenjoren, Maxi Data,Windows World; SWITZERLAND'S Computerworld Schweiz, Macworld Schweiz, PC Tip; TAIWAN'S Computerworld Taiwan, PC World Taiwan; THAILAND'S Thai Computerworld; TURKEY'S Computerworld Monitor, Macworld Turkiye, PC World Turkiye; UKRAINE'S Computerworld, Computers+Software Magazine; UNITED KINGDOM'S Computing /Computerworld, Connexion/Network World, Lotus Magazine, Macworld, Open Computing/Sunworld; URAGUAY'S PC World Uraguay; UNITED STATES' Advanced Systems, AmigaWorld, Cable in the Classroom, CD Review, CIO, Computerworld, Computerworld Client/Server Journal, Digital Video, DOS World, Electronic Entertainment Magazine (E2), Federal Computer Week, Game Hits, GamePro, IDG Books, Infoworld, Laser Event, Macworld, Maximize, Multimedia World, Network World, PC Letter, PC World, Publish, SWATPro, Video Event; VENEZUELA'S Computerworld Venezuela, PC World; VIETNAM'S PC World Vietnam. 11-16-94

Credits

Exec. VP, Strategic Product Planning & Research
David Solomon

Acquisitions Editor
Megg Bonar

Brand Manager
Judith A. Taylor

Editorial Director
Diane Graves Steele

Editorial Managers
Tracy L. Barr
Sandra Blackthorn

Editorial Assistants
Tamara S. Castleman
Stacey Holden Prince
Kevin Spencer

Acquisitions Assistant
Suki Gear

Production Director
Beth Jenkins

Associate Project Coordinator
Valery Bourke

Pre-Press Coordinator
Steve Peake

Associate Project Editor
A. Timothy Gallan

Technical Reviewer
Dennis Cohen

Production Staff
Paul Belcastro
Linda M. Boyer
Chris Collins
J. Tyler Connor
Maridee Ennis
Mark Owens
Carla Radzikinas
Dwight Ramsey
Patricia R. Reynolds
Gina Scott

Proofreader
Betty Kish

Indexer
Sharon Hilgenberg

Acknowledgments

First, before all others, I want to thank those who gave me the strength to get through all of this. A special thanks to Bjoern for typing, editing, and generally just being there, and to all of our friends for their support. I'd like to dedicate this book to Lee Hay, who first taught me poetry (which I still can't remember) and who has already gotten her PowerMac while I'm still waiting for mine.

There are also a number of people at IDG who deserve thanks. Tim Gallan did an outstanding job managing the project, improving my voice, and catching my lapses. Dennis Cohen reviewed the book for technical accuracy; any remaining mistakes are my own. The project could never have gotten off the ground without help from Megg Bonar who originally contacted me. For me, the greatest thanks must go to Suki Gear who makes sure my checks actually go to the right address. In addition, I'd like to thank Diane Steele who continues to listen to my problems and more importantly, tries to resolve them. Finally, I need to thank Mark Owens, who is responsible for the fact that you're seeing this book in its published form with all of the icons neatly in place, and Sharon Hilgenberg who compiled the index, which should make it easier for you to find things.

Contents at a Glance

Introduction

Well, let's try this again. Reader, I'd like you to meet the *Macintosh System 7.5 For Dummies Quick Reference*. *Quick Ref*, I'd like you to meet the reader.

What's This Book All About?

Now that the introductions are out of the way, we can get down to business. System 7.5, Apple's most recent upgrade to the Macintosh's operating system, contains a few entirely new and major features in addition to a wide variety of small improvements. The purpose of the *Macintosh System 7.5 For Dummies Quick Reference* is to give you a single source to answer all of your questions about using System 7.5. It's not meant to be a tutorial on the new operating system; nor is it an introduction to the Macintosh. (There are other *...For Dummies* titles for those purposes.) When using this book, the key is knowing how to find what you need.

The first part of the book contains "63 Things To Do With Your Mouse — The Clean Version" and lists many of the common tasks you'll perform on your Mac. The tasks are alphabetized within broad categories and are listed in the index (many under more than one entry). For some of the tasks, you're cross-referenced to the second part of the book, the "Command Reference," where each of the menu commands in the Finder is described in detail. These two sections cover all of the basic things you need to know about using your Mac, and you'll also find information about many of the minor changes in System 7.5 (carefully marked with the New icon). Some of major new features are discussed specifically in later parts.

Part 3, "Stop Mousing Around — Use Your Keyboard," reveals some surprisingly useful Macintosh tricks that don't require the mouse. Part 4, "Comfortable Customizing with Control Panels" and Part 5, "Puzzling Out the Extensions," give you an overview of the various components of System 7.5. These components give your Mac additional functionality (extensions), and they allow you to customize your Mac environment (control panels).

Part 6, "Acting Lessons: Using Scripts," introduces one of the major changes in System 7.5 — the addition of a scripting language, which enables you to create your own programs using commands from the desktop and even some programs.

In Part 7, "Printing Perfection," I cover just about everything you need to know about printing from your Macintosh, both the old way and with the new QuickDraw GX. I even explain what QuickDraw GX is and how to use it.

Part 8, "Playing Post Office with PowerTalk," details the new mail features that are built into System 7.5 as well as many AppleTalk and collaborative networking features. This part is a must-read for anyone who uses an Apple network. Of course, one of the reasons for putting all of this info in a separate section is that if you don't have a network, you can just skip right over it.

Finally, the last part in the book, "Taking It with You: PowerBook Features," covers those features that only appear if the Mac you are using is a PowerBook. There are a whole bunch of items including some controls panels, an extension or two, and even a special program for keeping your files organized.

For such a small book, I think I've managed to cover quite a lot. I hope you enjoy reading it and that it gives you the answers you need to make the most of your Mac.

What Do Those Pesky Icons Mean?

This book is filled with funny little pictures designed to make comprehension a little easier. These pictures are called icons. The following list tells you what they signify:

This icon flags commands and tasks that are recommended for the average Mac user.

This icon points out commands and tasks that are not recommended for the average Mac user.

This icon designates the kind of command or task that an average Mac user may not want to use, but learning this information may come in handy.

This icon flags commands and tasks that you can safely use.

This icon flags commands and tasks that are usually safe, but if you're not careful, you may run into trouble.

This icon designates commands and tasks that pose some danger to your data if you make a mistake, so be careful. You may be better off having someone else perform the commands and tasks marked with this icon.

This icon points out commands and tasks that you should never use unless you're some kind of programmer or technical guru.

This icon warns of problem areas and potentially dangerous situations.

This icon points out stuff that's, well, noteworthy.

This icon flags helpful information that will make life with your Mac easier (and maybe more fun).

This icon indicates a feature or component available only on Power Macs.

This icon helps you find the new and improved features in System 7.5.

This icon indicates a cross-reference to another entry or section within this Quick Reference.

This icon flags cross-references to material in IDG's *Macintosh System 7.5 For Dummies,* by Bob LeVitus.

Part 1

63 Things To Do with Your Mouse — The Clean Version

Sometimes it's not enough to know what each command in a program does — you need to know how to do something. This section lists in alphabetical order the various activities on and around the desktop that require mouse movement. This part could almost have the subtitle "System 7.5 Basics" because it describes the everyday actions that all users need to know in order to work with their Macs.

Of course, we needed a way to organize them for the book. I've first grouped them into major headings based upon what you are working with. For example, I've tried to group everything you need to know about working with a file in a section called "File Things." But that left me with still needing an order for the headings themselves and a way to organize the items within each heading. Because all editors and writers spent so much time staring at dictionaries, we decided to alphabetize the entires. Of course, you can always just flip through to find something or look it up in the index. The activities referenced in this part are listed in the following categories:

- Desktop things
- Disk things
- File things
- Folder things
- Icon things
- List things
- Window things

There's one group that deserves special mention. Icon Things covers just those things that you might want to do while viewing icons within a window. Many of the things you do with files and folders can be done by manipulating the icon, but I've covered them in their own sections rather than with those things you do while viewing an icon.

(By the way, if you'd like the dirty version of "63 Things To Do with Your Mouse," write to IDG Books in care of Tim Gallan and maybe he'll let me put that section in a future edition of this book.)

Desktop Things

The desktop is the background that you see when you are working with the Finder. You can tell you are working with the Finder when the icon in the upper-right corner of the menu bar looks like a little tiny Macintosh. Another good clue is that all of the menus that are talked about in this handy reference are available when you're in the Finder (such as View, Label and Special). If you're running other programs, the desktop still appears as the background unless you specify otherwise in the General Controls control panel.

With earlier versions of the System, the disk icons and the Trash on your desktop were always visible (unless they were behind a window). It didn't matter whether you were working in another program; the desktop icons were still there. With System 7.5, you have the option of hiding the icons that are on the desktop while you work in a different program. In the General Controls control panel, you can uncheck the Show Desktop when in background option if you would like to hide the desktop while working in another application. Although they are often considered part of the desktop, some of the things in the menu bar, such as the Apple menu, the date and time display, and portions of the Guide menu (a.k.a. the ? menu) are available in all programs whether you've hidden the desktop or not.

Checking what's in the Trash

Sometimes, you may realize that there's something in the Trash, but you're not sure what it is. You may look down and discover that it's bulging and you don't remember putting anything into it, or you may start to empty it and realize that the number or size of the items in the Trash doesn't sound right.

The first thing you should know is how to tell if there's anything at all in the Trash. If the Trash is empty, it has a slim, straight-sided look like the one on the left in the following figure. If there's anything at all in the Trash, it's sides bulge in a most unbecoming way like the one on right.

To find out what's in the Trash, point to the Trash and double-click. The Trash window appears showing the items contained in the Trash. Remember that any folders in the Trash may contain other items.

If there's something in the Trash that you decide you want to keep, just put your cursor over it, hold down the mouse button, and drag it onto the desktop or into another folder. You can move a single file or an entire folder.

NOTE: Fairly often, strange things may appear in your Trash. For example, if you cancel a print job, the printing file is put into the Trash. Also, if your system crashes, you may get a folder of "rescued" items. If the size of these items is zero, you can safely throw them away. If the items are actual files, you may have to remove them from the Trash to see what they are. Always check the contents of folders you don't recognize. If the name of a file or folder seem very strange (particularly if it's mostly numbers or random letters), it was probably a temporary file created by one of your programs, and it's OK to toss it out. Files that end with the word *print* are put into the Trash when you are using QuickDraw GX and you cancel a print job. These files are copies of the original that you were printing and are OK to throw away.

REFERENCE: For more information about working with the Trash window, see "Window Things." You may find it easier to list the things that are in the Trash using the techniques discussed in "List Things."

Cleaning up the desktop

Don't you just hate it when the papers on your desk get so high that you can't see over them anymore? Well, I can't do anything about that problem, but I can show you how to clean up the icons on your desktop.

The first step is to make the desktop active. (No, it won't jump up on your desk and do aerobic exercises.) Hold down the ⌘ key and the Shift keys and press the Up Arrow. This action deselects any active window and makes the desktop active. Next, choose Special⇨Clean Up Desktop, and all of the icons on your desktop will jump to attention and line up on the grid, just like files or folders within a window.

NOTE: If you hold down the Option key while the desktop is active, you can select Special⇨Clean Up All. This command causes all of the icons to move over to the right side of your screen and line up in neat columns.

REFERENCE: For more on how the Clean Up command works, you can either look at "Lining up those icons" in the "Icon Things" section of this part or look up Special⇨Clean Up in Part 2.

Emptying the Trash

If you have something in the Trash that you want to actually remove from the disk, it's fairly easy to get rid of it. Just make sure that everything that's in the Trash really is something you want to toss out.

To empty the Trash, select Special⇨Empty Trash. You get a dialog box that tells you how many items are in the Trash and their total size. If you're confident that you aren't going to throw out something you need, click OK. If the Special⇨Empty Trash command isn't available (that is, it's grayed out), then the Trash is already empty.

Always take a moment to actually read the dialog box message. If the numbers it reports are very different from what you expect, you should probably check what's in the Trash before emptying. For example, if you threw out a single document that contained a two-page letter and the dialog box is reporting seven items that take up 1.5MB, you'd better check what those other six items are.

If the Trash contains objects that are locked, you can force your Macintosh to throw them away by holding down the Option key while you choose Special⇨Empty Trash. On the other hand, take a moment and ask yourself why those files were locked in the first place. Maybe you threw them out once before and discovered they really were important.

If, like most users, you get really annoyed by the warning dialog box every time you go to empty the Trash, you can turn it off and never have to deal with it again (just be careful when you're emptying the Trash). Click the Trash to select it. Choose the Get Info command from the File menu. In the resulting Trash Info window, uncheck the Warn before emptying check box.

To find out how to deliberately put things into the Trash, see "Deleting a file" in File Things.

Hiding all the other programs

One of the problems with working on more than one program at oncc is that the desktop can become very cluttered. The clutter is even harder to handle if you are working with a program that uses only a small portion of the screen, such as Calculator. It's often convenient to hide all of the other programs so that they don't distract you.

Admittedly, hiding a program isn't strictly a mouse technique (it uses a menu), but it is important. You need to start from the program you want to keep working in. Move your cursor over the icon at the far right of the menu bar (the Application menu), hold down the mouse button, and choose Hide Others from the Application menu.

A hidden program is still running; you just can't see it. To unhide hidden program windows, go to the Application menu and choose Show All.

NOTE

The other command on the top part of the Application menu hides the current program. This command's name changes depending on the program. For example, if you're in the Finder, the command is Hide Finder; if you're in Microsoft Word, it's Hide Microsoft Word.

Hiding the current program when you switch to another

If you're switching from a program that takes up most of the screen to one that is in a much smaller window, you may want to hide the large program as you leave it. Otherwise, the larger window will be in the background and can be quite distracting. Hiding programs can also help you keep your job: you can quickly hide that new game and switch to the Finder when your boss knocks on your door.

To hide the current program as you switch to another, hold down the Option key when you select the new program from the Application menu.

Hiding the desktop when you start a program

NEW 7.5

Probably one of the most useful new features in System 7.5 is the capability to hide the icons that are on the desktop when you're not in the Finder. The various icons on the desktop — the icons representing disks, the Trash, and any folders or files — are absolutely necessary when you're working with the Finder. How could you copy a file to a disk without a disk icon? On the other hand, those icons can be very distracting when they're peeking out from behind the windows of another program.

Whether the icons disappear when you move to another program is a feature of the General Controls control panel. To turn on the feature, choose Apple menu⇨Control Panels⇨General Controls. If there is a check next to the Show Desktop when in background option, then the icons are visible regardless of which program you're in, which is the way earlier versions of the System behaved (or misbehaved, depending upon your viewpoint). If you clear the check box (by clicking on it so that the check disappears), moving from the Finder to another program will hide the desktop icons.

NOTE

With the icons hidden, you cannot switch back to the Finder by clicking on the desktop. You have to use the Application menu just like you do when moving to another program.

REFERENCE

You can find out more about what the General Controls control panel controls by checking out its entry in Part 5, "Comfortable Customizing with Control Panels."

Playing audio CDs

NEW 7.5

If your Macintosh has a CD-ROM drive attached, you can listen to an audio CD while you work. Most Macintoshes have a built-in speaker through which you can play music, but the sound quality isn't nearly as good as that produced by a decent set of stereo speakers.

To get started, choose Apple menu⇨AppleCD Audio Player. A window should appear on your screen with what looks like the front of a car stereo. Place an audio CD into the drive. When you close the drive (and your Macintosh gets around to reading the CD), the indicator window (in the upper-left corner) displays Track 01 and Elapsed Time 00:00. If you've played the CD before and you've provided the CD's title, the title of the CD appears in the upper-right. Otherwise, the display will read *Audio CD* followed by a number.

To play the tracks on the CD in order (from track 1 through to the end), click the Play button (it has a right-pointing triangle on it). You can adjust the volume using the slide bar at the right of the window. Move the lever up to increase the volume and down to lower the volume. In addition, you may be able to adjust the sound directly on your speakers. (To play the tracks in a random order, click on the Shuffle button on the left of the window.)

To temporarily pause the CD, click the same button you used to start playing. It's now the Pause button, and its symbol is two parallel lines. To restart the music, press the button again. (It's now the Play button again.) To stop the CD, press the Stop button to the left of the Pause/Play button. It's the one with a solid square within it.

Putting stickies on your desktop

NEW 7.5

The easiest way to get a note on your desktop is to use a real Post-it-style note and stick it on the edge of your monitor. Of course, this tends to upset the office guru, so maybe you'd better use the electronic ones after all. By the way, most of the menu commands refer to stickies as *notes,* but the program is called Stickies, and I like that name better. So I use *stickie* or *stickies* to refer to the notes on your screen, but the names for commands are exactly as they appear on the menu.

To get started with Stickies, choose Apple menu⇨Stickies. Any Stickies that already exist appear on your screen. If you've never used Stickies before, three appear by default when you open Stickies for the first time. They explain the very basics of using this desk accessory. If you have a blank stickie, just click inside its window and type your note. If there aren't any blank ones, choose File⇨New Note and then start typing.

To change the format of a stickie, you use the Note and Color menus. Make sure that your cursor is in the stickie you want to change. (You can tell which stickie you're in because it has a title bar and window controls.) To change the background color, simply choose the new color from the Color menu. To change the font for that stickie, choose Note⇨Text Style, make your selections in the dialog box, and then click OK. If you come up with a text style and color combination that you particularly like, you can have all of your new stickies created using that format by choosing Edit⇨Use As Default. Make sure that you're in the stickie you like before choosing the command.

To find out when a stickie was created and last modified, select the stickie and then choose Note⇨Note Info.

To change the contents of a stickie, you can use any of the standard editing commands (Cut, Copy and Paste), as well as File⇨Import Text (to bring text in from another file) and File⇨Export Text (to place the text from a stickie into a file).

To print a single stickie, select that stickie and then choose File⇨Print Note. If you want to print all of your notes, choose File⇨Print All Notes. Generally, you'll just need to click OK in the resulting Print dialog box and you're all set.

If you need help with any print options, see File⇨Print in Part 2.

To get rid of a stickie, simply close it by clicking in the close box in the upper-right corner of the stickie. If there's anything within the stickie, you'll get a dialog box warning you that you're about to lose that information. You can throw the contents away by clicking Don't Save. You can save the text to a separate file by clicking Save. If you didn't mean to close the stickie and want to keep it, click Cancel. If you close a stickie by mistake and realize it immediately, you can use Edit⇨Undo to bring it back.

To stop using Stickies and clear all of them from your screen, choose File⇨Quit. Normally, stickies are automatically saved when you stop working with them. If you want to be absolutely sure about saving everything, choose File⇨Save All before quitting Stickies. If File⇨Save All isn't available, you haven't made any changes, so there's nothing to save.

If you really like Stickies and want to use them all the time, select Edit⇨Preferences and put a check next to the option "Launch at system startup."

Stickies are actually in little tiny windows, and even though the controls in the corners look slightly different, you can still use them for zooming, resizing, and moving the window. Just remember that if you close a stickie, its text is gone!

Showing the date or time

With System 7.5, Apple finally acknowledged that people might have something better to do with their lives than sit around and work on the computer all the time. That is why the current time (or the current date) is displayed in the menu bar at the top of your screen.

You can easily switch between seeing the date and seeing the time by clicking on whichever one is showing. If you click on the date, you'll see the time. If you click on the time, you'll see the date. You have to admit there's a certain logic to it all.

You can control the format for the date and time by using the Date & Time control panel. Click the Clock Options button in this control panel to access, you guessed it, the clock options.

Switching between programs

Working with more than one program at a time is a great timesaver, but this capability does add a degree of complexity to the Mac environment. To help you keep your programs and their windows organized, Apple provides a menu dedicated solely to working with the various programs, or *applications,* that you are currently using.

The Application menu is probably the most difficult menu for most people to find because its icon keeps changing. It's the far-right menu on the menu bar. If you are in the Finder, the icon looks like a little Macintosh; if you are in another program, the icon is the miniature version of the icon for that program.

To use the Application menu, point to its icon (whatever it looks like) and hold down the mouse button. At the bottom of the menu is a list of all of the programs that are currently running. Move down the menu until the program that you want to use is highlighted. Then release the mouse button. Your Macintosh will switch over to that program and let you get on with your work.

If the program you want to work with isn't on the Application menu, you'll have to go back to the Finder and open the program you want to use.

There's another, very evil way to move between programs. It's evil because so many people do it by accident. If you can see part of a window or an icon that belongs to another program, clicking on that object will move you to the other program. If you find yourself constantly moving to the desktop by accident, you can use the General Controls control panel to hide the desktop, which means that you have to use the Application menu to move to the Finder.

Turning off your Macintosh

You should use the Special⇨Shut Down command before turning off your Macintosh. When you choose Shut Down, your Macintosh closes any programs you are using, making sure that all of the files you have been using are properly stored and that any changes you have made have been recorded.

NEW 7.5

With System 7.5, there are two ways to get to the Shut Down command. You can either return to the desktop and choose Special⇨Shut Down or choose Apple menu⇨•Shut Down from within any program.

No matter which command you choose, your Mac begins closing any programs that you have been using. For each program, your Mac checks to see whether you have made any changes that haven't been saved. If so, it asks you whether you want to save the changes. If you click No, the changes are thrown out. If you click Yes, the file is saved normally. If you click Cancel, the shut down procedure is canceled at that point and you can go back to using your Mac.

Next, your Mac makes sure that all of the files have been stored properly and updates it's own records of where files are stored. In addition, it stores information about which windows were open and how the screen was arranged. Finally, it shuts down the system. On many models, this means that the power is actually turned off for you. On other, usually lower-priced models, however, you just get a message telling you that it's OK to turn the power off yourself.

TIP

You can use the Warn me if computer was shut down improperly option in the General Controls control panel to have your Mac tell you if someone turned it off without using the Shut Down command. Great. Now, your Mac is turning into a tattletale.

Turning the power off or on automatically

NEW 7.5

If your computer is connected to a network, there may be times when you need to turn it on or off when you're not planning on being there. With Auto Power On/Off, you can set your computer to turn off at a specific time. If your system is connected to a modem and you travel, you may want to have your computer turn on at a specific time so that you can call and connect to your system to get messages or update your files.

The Auto Power On/Off control panel is actually quite easy to use. There are separate sections for turning your computer on and off, but they work the same way. The only thing that might possibly cause confusion is the choice between Once and Recurring. Use the Once option if you want to control your computer at a single specific time. Use the Recurring option when you want to control your Macintosh at the same time every week.

If you wanted to make sure that your computer is turned on for the start of the new year, you'd check the Once box in the Turn the computer on section. Then click on the month in the first box and enter **12** (either by just typing it or by using the arrows on the right). Next, click on the day and enter **31**. Finally, click on the parts of the time in the second box and change them to read **11**, **59** and **PM**. You can now turn your Mac off and it will restart all by itself just before midnight on New Year's eve.

If you often forget to turn your computer off in the rush to go home, you might set the Auto Power On/Off control panel so that it turns your Mac off every work day at 6 p.m. Just click the Recurring box in the Turn the computer off section. Then choose the Weekdays option from the drop-down list and enter **6:00 PM** as the time in the second box. Your computer will turn itself off every weekday at 6 p.m.

If your computer is on a network, you should probably also check the Warn _ minutes before shut down box and specify how many minutes of warning to give users who are connected via file sharing to your Mac.

Finally, you can use the Automatically restart after power failure option to have your computer automatically restart when the power is turned back on following a power failure. This feature is useful if you want your computer to be on all the time.

NOTE

For years, computer users have debated whether it's a good idea to turn off your computer when you are away from your desk. Most people agree about the monitor — either turn it off or use a screen saver program — but there is disagreement about whether turning your system (particularly your hard disk) on and off causes it to wear out faster. I don't have the definitive answer, but I use a screen saver that comes on after three minutes of inactivity, and I turn my computer off if I'm going to be away from it for more than a day or two. Of course, with the schedule IDG has given me, I have a little chain that runs from my ankle to the computer, but that's a different story.

WARNING!

Unfortunately, the Auto Power On/Off control panel doesn't work on all systems.

Using desktop clippings

NEW 7.5

System 7.5 introduces the new Macintosh Drag and Drop technology for moving information between programs. Previously, you could store something in the Scrapbook for use in any program, or you could use the Cut, Copy, and Paste commands to move things between programs. With the Macintosh Drag and Drop technology, you can store bits and pieces of a document directly on the desktop or within folders. These document elements are called *clippings,* and they can be used with any program capable of working with the new technology.

To create a clipping, you need to start in the document that contains the information. If you want to practice, you can use the Scrapbook. First, adjust your window so you can see the background of the desktop. You don't need to be able to see any of the desktop icons. Highlight whatever you want to clip and drag it to the desktop. When you release the mouse button, your Mac creates a clipping file. The original information is left in the document.

To view a clipping, double-click on the clipping file. Your Macintosh finds an appropriate program (such as SimpleText) and opens the program with the clipping. Some clippings just display by themselves (such as pictures), and others you can't really see (such as sounds), but you can still use all of them in your documents.

To use a clipping, you need to be running a program that uses the new Macintosh Drag and Drop. If you just want to practice, Notebook is a good choice. To add a clipping to a document, drag the clipping file from its origin to the document. When you release the mouse button, the contents of the clipping file are placed in the document.

NOTE

All of the old-fashioned ways of moving information between programs still work. You can put something into the Scrapbook so that it's always available on the Apple menu, and you can use the Cut, Copy, and Paste commands to move or copy information between programs via the Clipboard.

WARNING!

To use clippings, you need to be able to see the desktop icons. That means you either have to work with them in the Finder or be sure you are not hiding the desktop when you start a program, as discussed earlier in this section.

Disk Things

Disks are probably the most important part of your computer system because you use them to store your work and your applications. There are several different types of disks, but your Macintosh can recognize them all and arranges them in a neat line down the right side of your screen. The icons shown here are for several of the most common types of disks.

The icon on the far right isn't really a disk but a folder on someone else's computer. I show it here because you treat it exactly like another disk.

For more information about System 7.5's nifty new and neat network features, see Part 8.

Copying a floppy disk onto your hard disk

It's quite easy to copy an entire floppy disk onto your hard disk. Insert the floppy into your Mac. Drag the disk icon onto your hard disk icon and release the mouse button. Your Mac realizes that you are copying an entire floppy. It creates a folder on your hard disk with the same name as the floppy disk and puts the contents of the floppy disk into that folder.

Duplicating an entire disk

You duplicate a disk when you need a second copy. Perhaps you have a disk you want to share with a friend, or maybe you're creating a backup disk for safety.

With two floppy disk drives, you put the original in one disk drive and another disk in the second disk drive. Preferably, the second disk is either a new or at least empty disk of the same size. If there is anything on the second disk, it will be deleted when you copy the first disk on top of it. If the disk in the second drive isn't formatted, you'll be asked to format it at this time. If you need help, see the section "Formatting a disk." By the way, it doesn't matter which drive you count as the first and which is the second as long as you remember which one has the original. To actually copy the disk, put your cursor over the icon for the original disk, press and hold your mouse button, and move the outline of the disk onto the second disk. When you are in the right position, the second disk will darken, and when you release the mouse button, you get a dialog box asking you to confirm that you mean to replace the contents of the second disk with a copy of the original disk. Click OK, wait a moment or two, and you have two identical disks.

If you only have one disk drive, the process is a bit tougher. Insert the original disk and then choose Special⇨Eject Disk. The disk will pop out of your machine, but the disk icon will stay on the desktop (with a ghostly-gray shading). Insert the second disk. Put your cursor over the icon for the first disk, hold down the mouse button, and move the cursor so that it is over the icon for the second disk. When you release the mouse button, your Macintosh will ask you to confirm that you really want to replace anything that is on the second disk with a copy of what was on the first. Click OK to continue and then dance the amazing disk swap duet. In this duet, your Macintosh ejects one disk and asks you to insert the other. It may happen only once, or you may get to swap seven or eight times. Eventually, the disk will be copied and you can drag both of the disk icons to the Trash to eject them from your Macintosh.

TIP

Often, if you only have one disk drive, it is easier to copy all of the contents of the original disk into a folder on your hard disk and then copy that onto a second disk.

Ejecting a disk

You can't just leave all of your disks stuck inside of your computer, so you have to eject them sooner or later, and there are two different ways to eject a disk. The first causes your Macintosh to forget that the disk was ever around in the first place. The second leaves the icons for the disk on the desktop but frees up the disk drive so that you can insert another disk.

To eject a disk and have your Macintosh forget all about it, put your cursor over the disk icon, hold down the mouse button, and move the cursor over the Trash. When you release the mouse button, the disk pops out of the disk drive and the disk icon disappears. Don't worry about putting the disk into the Trash — it doesn't erase anything from the disk. You can also use the Put Away command in the File menu to eject a disk in the same way.

To eject a disk but leave the disk icon on the desktop, click the disk and choose Special⇨Eject Disk. The disk pops out but the icon remains in place. To get rid of the icon, you have to drag it to the Trash. Don't worry if you are throwing out a disk icon and your Macintosh asks you to reinsert the disk. It just needs to do some final housekeeping before getting rid of the icon.

Erasing a disk

There are two different things that people mean when they talk about erasing a disk. One is just emptying it out so that there's nothing on it. The other is reformatting it. Most of the time, you just need to throw away the contents to reuse a disk. I find that constantly reformatting a disk makes it more likely to wear out.

To throw out everything that is on a disk, first double-click the disk icon. A window opens showing the disk's contents. Choose Edit⇨Select All. With all of the disk's contents selected, put your cursor over any of the highlighted items, press and hold the mouse button, and drag the cursor over the Trash. When the Trash darkens (indicating that you're in the right position to throw something away), release the mouse button. For the final step, choose Special⇨Empty Trash.

To reformat a disk, select the disk by clicking on it once and then choose Special⇨Erase Disk. Your Mac will walk you through the steps of reformatting the disk. For more details, see this command's entry in Part 2.

Formatting a disk

You need to format a disk before you can put any information onto it. You can think of an unformatted disk as being a blank sheet of paper — it's very difficult to write on neatly. On the other hand, a formatted disk is like ruled paper with little lines to guide your writing. Your Macintosh needs the markers that are put on a formatted disk to know where to store information.

Formatting disks was one of the things that made the early Macintoshes seem so much simpler than their DOS counterparts. On the Macintosh, you simply put the disk into the disk drive. If the disk isn't formatted, your Mac tells you that the disk is unreadable, and it asks you whether you want to *initialize* it. Initialize is just another word for formatting.

NEW 7.5

The dialog box has a drop-down list which lets you decide what format to use. The details of the formatting choices are covered under Special⇨Erase Disk in Part 2. Fortunately, 95 percent of the time, you just want to take the choice that your Mac suggests. You should also type in a name for the disk. It's really annoying to end up with seven or eight disks all named "untitled." Once you're sure of the name and the format, click on the Initialize button. You then get another dialog box warning you that "Initializing will erase all information on this disk." Assuming you want to go ahead with everything, either click the Continue button or press Return. Your disk drive churns for a while and eventually a disk icon for the newly formatted disk appears on your desktop. You now have your very own formatted disk.

TIP

If you just want to get rid of all of the information from the disk, open the disk and drag all of the contents to the Trash. Then select Special⇨Empty Trash to actually get rid of the contents. If you just drag the disk icon to the Trash, you'll eject the disk.

REFERENCE

For more information on the options available when formatting a disk, see the Special⇨Erase Disk command in Part 2.

Opening a disk

You need to open a disk to see what's inside of it. Even though it's quite tempting, don't try prying the two sides of the plastic disk apart; there's an easier way.

In fact, there are two easier ways. You can double click a disk icon to open it. And you can click once on a disk icon to select it and choose File⇨Open.

Renaming a disk

Changing the name for a disk is basically the same as changing the name of a file or a folder. The first step is to select the disk's name and only the name. To select the name, click once over the file name and then leave your cursor in the same position. After a moment, the background of the name should change from black to your highlight color. That's your signal that you're ready to edit the name. You can now just type the new name or edit the old one.

File Things

File Things have to do with working with a single file, whether you're moving it as an icon or working with its contents by printing it. All of the following are samples of icons that represent files.

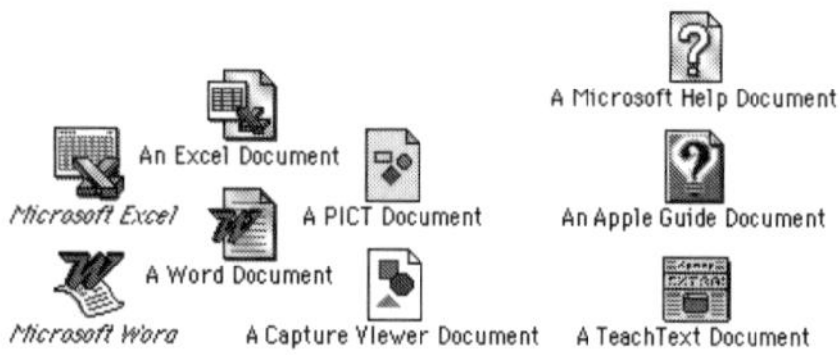

Most things that you can do with a single file (including printing), you can do with a group of files. The techniques for working with a group are described in "Moving a group of files" in this section.

If what you want to do is change the way the icons representing the files are arranged within the window, you should look at the topics under "Icon Things." If you want to organize a window that is showing a list of files and folders, see "List Things." To move, copy or otherwise deal with a folder and all of its contents, see "Folder Things."

Changing a file's name

You generally change names to protect the innocent or because you realize that "FL94RPT" really isn't as easy to remember as you thought it would be and that maybe "Fall 94 Report" would be a better choice.

Select the file's name and only the name (and it's harder than you think) by clicking once over the file name and then leaving the cursor in the same position. After a moment, the background of the name should change from black to your highlight color. That's your signal that you're ready to edit the name. (You can also click once and then press Return for the same effect.)

There are three basic editing techniques. The least sophisticated, but easiest, is to press Delete and just type the new name. The second is to highlight what you want to change and type in the new information. You can double-click to highlight a word and drag to highlight a selection. The final method is to click once where you want to insert characters (just start typing after the background turns white). You can also click to the right of characters you want to remove and use the Delete key to get rid of characters to the left of where you are.

You can also use the Edit⇨Cut, Edit⇨Copy and Edit⇨Paste commands to reuse all or part of another file's name. Just be aware that two files in the same folder can't have the same name.

Some items have names that can't be changed. These include your mailbox, the name of a CD, and any files on a CD.

The only character you can't use in a file's name is the colon (:). Your Macintosh uses the colon to connect the names of the disk and any folders to the file name. If you see something like "Macintosh HD:Documents:IDG:New Book," it means that the file "New Book" in the folder "IDG" which is in the folder "Documents" on the disk "Macintosh HD." Most people use the dash in place of the colon when they create document names. So instead of *Financial Report: June,* you use *Financial Report-June.*

You can put a space at the start of a name to make a file appear at the top of file lists. You can use other symbols (such as the bullet made with Option-8) to make a file appear at the bottom of a list.

Copying a file to a different disk

You'll need to copy a file to another disk when you want to share it with a friend or to create a *backup* — a copy of a file that you keep in a safe place.

The icon for the disk that you are aiming for should be one of the ones along the right side of your screen. If it's a floppy disk, make sure the disk is inserted into the machine before you begin. Find the file that you want to copy and place the cursor over it. Press and hold down the mouse button and move the cursor (along with the outline of the file) over the disk's icon. The icon will darken and the background for the disk's name will turn black to show you when you're in the right position. Lift up on the button and your Macintosh will begin copying.

Copying a file is the first step in moving a file from one disk to another. To finish moving, you need to go back and delete the original. You would do this to free up room on the disk from which you copied the original file. Unfortunately, there is no way to move a file to another disk in a single step. When you're done copying a file you want to move, you have two identical files — one on the original disk and new one on the second disk. If you want, you can now go back and delete the original off of the disk you started from. Of course, it never hurts to keep a backup around in case of an accident.

NOTE

If you only have a single disk drive and you are trying to copy a file from one floppy disk to another, you have two options:

- Copy the file twice — once to your hard disk and then from your hard disk to the second floppy.
- Insert the disk with the file you want to copy. Open the disk's window so that the file is visible. Select the disk by clicking it's icon; then choose Special⇨Eject Disk. Insert the second disk and drag the file from it's window onto the second disk. You may have to keep switching back and forth between your two disks in order to complete the copy. Don't worry, your Macintosh will eject each disk and ask you for the one it wants.

Copying a file to a different folder

You might want to keep a separate copy of a file for archival reasons (you might need to go back to it) or for safety reasons (a *backup* so that if your original is damaged you have another chance).

The steps for copying a file to a different folder are remarkably similar to those for putting a file into a folder. The only difference is that you hold down the Option key as you drag the file. First, you need to be able to see both the file you want to copy and the folder where you want the copy. Next, put the arrow cursor over the file, press and hold down the mouse button, and drag the cursor over to the folder. Don't worry if the folder is in another window. When the cursor is in the right position, the folder will darken and its name will get a black background. Now, to make your copy, hold down the Option key while you release the mouse button. A dialog box appears, indicating that a file is being copied.

NOTE

Some people find it much easier to just press the Option key when they first select the file and hold it down throughout the entire process of moving the file. Either way works as long as you have the Option key down when you release the mouse button.

NOTE

If you realize that you are copying the wrong file (or group of files), click the Stop button in the Copy dialog box.

TIP

If a file with the same name already exists in the folder to which you are copying, a dialog box appears asking you whether or not you want to replace the one in the folder with the one that you are copying. This dialog box will tell you whether the file in the folder is older or newer than the file you are copying. (If the two files are the same age, the dialog box won't mention anything about it.) If you click OK in the dialog box, the file in the folder will be replaced. If you click Cancel, the file will not be copied. (If you are copying a group of files and click Cancel, no more files from that group will be copied.)

Although keeping a copy of a file in another folder offers some security, it's even better to keep a copy on another disk.

Deleting a file

Getting rid of a file requires two steps. First, drag the file into the Trash. In the lower-right corner of your screen is a little teeny tiny Trash. If the Trash was empty before you started, it's sides will now bulge to show you that there's something in there. Even if there is something else already in the Trash, you can add things, but the sides won't get any bigger.

The Trash is actually just a temporary storage place. Just like in real life, if you realize that you just threw out the note with an important address on it, you can open the Trash and look for it. To open the Trash, double-click it. Once you are sure that you don't want the stuff within the Trash, you can empty it: choose Special⇨Empty Trash. A dialog box appears telling you how many files are in the Trash and how much space they use. This is your last chance to change your mind. If you're still sure you want to throw out the contents of the Trash, click OK.

Delete locked files by holding down the Option key when choosing Special⇨Empty Trash.

You can move a group of files to the Trash at one time by selecting them together. The easiest way to select a small group is to click on the first file and then hold down the Shift key as you click on each additional file. When all the files are highlighted, put the cursor over any one of them to drag the whole group to the Trash.

For more information on the Trash, see "Checking what's in the Trash" in the "Desktop Things" section.

Duplicating (copying) a file to keep within the same folder

Select the file that you want to copy by clicking it once. Then choose File⇨Duplicate. A second file will appear with the same name as the original except that it ends with the word "copy." If you make a copy of a file that has a name that already ends with "copy," the new file will end with "copy 2."

File⇨Duplicate has a shortcut — ⌘-D. Just select the file, hold down the ⌘ key and press the letter D.

Finding a lost file

You've probably used the Find File command before, but the one that comes with System 7.5 is new and improved.

To get started, choose File⇨Find. You need to know something about the file you're looking for and the more you know, the more likely you are to find the right file. When you choose File⇨Find, you get the Find dialog box which has spaces for entering one bit of information about the file. The figure shows the options for enter-ing part of the files name, but you can also look for the file's size, kind, label, creation date, modification date, or some combination.

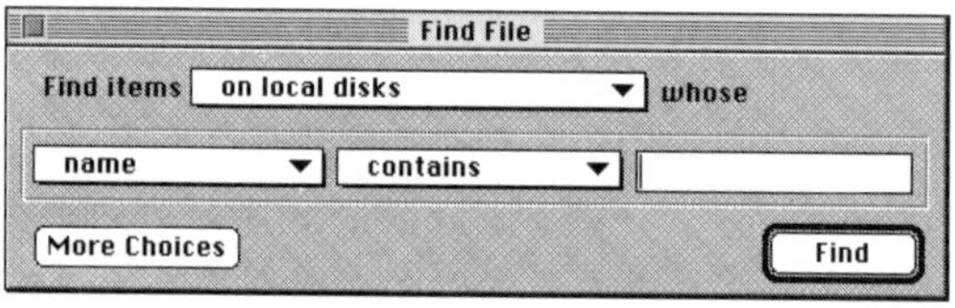

The phrase "or some combination" is crucial because each time you click on the More Choices button, you get another line with which you can search on a different characteristic. You can search for a file matching up to ten categories of information. The following figure shows these catagories.

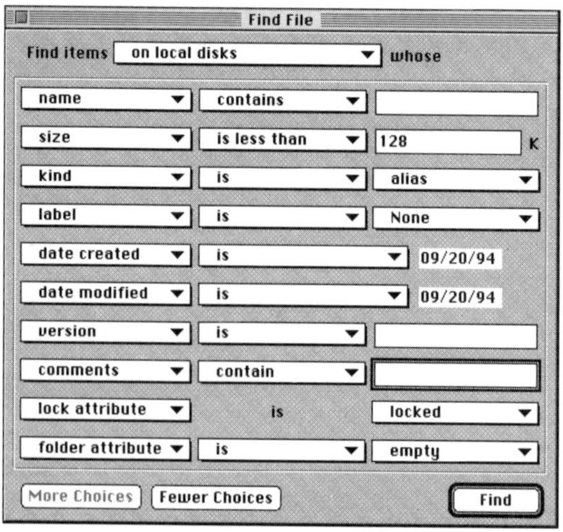

You use the various boxes in the dialog box to create a sentence telling your Macintosh what type of file to look for. Each line on the dialog box is connected with an "and whose." For example, your search might read "Find items on all disks whose name contains report and whose size is less than 512K."

For each choice, in the first column you select what characteristic about the file you want to match. If you know even part of the name, always use that as your first choice to help remind you of what you are looking for. You use the second column to describe how your Macintosh should compare the characteristic in the first column to the information the third column. The choices that are available change depending upon your selection in the first column. For example, with *Name* in the first column, the second column's choices are *contains* (the match is anywhere within the actual name), *starts with* (the match is at the beginning of the name), *ends with* (the match is at the end of the name), *is* (the name and the match are identical except for case), *is not* (the name is somehow different from the match), and *doesn't contain* (the match is not contained anywhere within the name). With *Size* selected in the first column, your second column choices are *is less than* or *is greater than*.

With most of the options in the first column, you can enter whatever you want into the third column as long as it makes sense for what you are searching. For example, if you are trying to match for size, you can enter any value. You can't have your Macintosh look for files whose size is less than "banana." For kind, label, lock attribute, and folder attribute, the third column contains a drop-down list of choices. With date created and date modified, you can click on the month, day, or year to change that part of the date in the third column.

At the very top of the dialog box is a drop-down list buried in the start of the sentence "Find items ... whose." The choices on that drop-down list complete the first part of the sentence and tell your Macintosh which disks to search.

After you've specified as many criteria as possible, click the Find button. The Find button turns into the Stop button, an entry appears at the bottom of the dialog box telling you how many items have been found, and a little pair of arrows chase each other in a circle on the right side of the dialog box. When all of the files that match your request are found, you get a new dialog box called Find File Results. As you can see in the next figure, the dialog box has two sections — a list of files on the top and the list of folders leading back to the desktop on the bottom.

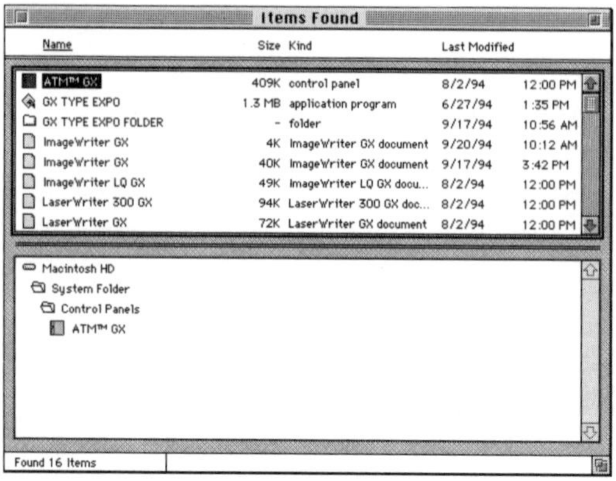

The bottom portion displays the location of the file selected in the top section. To find out where a file or folder is, click once on the name in the top section. To open the window containing a file from the list, double-click on the file's name. To open a folder that's on the list, double-click on its name. To move a file or folder, drag it from the list to the new location. You can move the split between the top and bottom sections by putting the cursor over the dividing bar, and when the cursor becomes a small hand, hold the mouse button and move the split to where you want it.

Because finding a file is unfortunately something that some of us have to do quite regularly, Apple has thoughtfully installed the same tool on the Apple menu. The only difference is that there it's called Find File. So, you can use File⇨Find when you are in the Finder and Apple menu⇨Find File whenever you want.

For more details on searching, see the entry for File⇨Find in Part 2.

Installing a file in the System Folder

There are certain types of files that must be placed in the System Folder in order for your Mac to work. In a perfect world, someone else would worry about what goes where in the System Folder. Unfortunately, as you may have noticed, it's not a perfect world.

The first step in putting a file into the System Folder is making sure that that's where the file belongs. The three most likely types of files that you need to place in the System Folder are extensions, control panels, or fonts. Fonts are usually pretty easy to identify because they look like little suitcases with letters on the side. Both control panels and extensions are discussed in their own chapters, but there's a relatively easy way to identify them. Click once on an icon to select it and then choose File⇨Get Info. The resulting Info window tells you what kind of file you're looking at.

To find your System Folder, double-click the hard disk icon in the upper-right corner of the desktop. In the window that opens, look for a folder with a little Macintosh on it and the name System Folder.

To move a file to the System Folder, drag its icon on top of the System Folder and release the mouse button. A message appears asking you whether you want your Macintosh to put the item in its proper folder within the System Folder. Make your machine do the work by clicking OK.

If you install an extension or control panel, you may need to restart your Mac before you can use that item. Simply choose Special⇨Restart.

Whenever possible, install control panels and extensions using the installation programs (if available) that accompany them. Many third-party control panels and extensions (as well as the ones that came with your Mac) have their own installation programs.

If you are installing things into the Apple Menu Items, Launcher, Startup Items, or Shutdown folder, you should create an alias of the item and put that into the folder. You install an original copy (not an alias) of a file if it goes into the Extensions, Control Panels, or Fonts folder.

If you happen to browse around within your System Folder, you may also find a few other types of files that are already in the Extension folder with file types such as shared library or Apple Guide document. These files have been installed by some of your programs and are fine where they are.

Control panels are discussed in Part 4; extensions are discussed in Part 5

Locking a file

If you have a file that is very important to you, locking it provides a simple way of making it harder to throw out. Be warned, however, that it isn't difficult to trash a locked file.

Click once on a file to select it and then choose File⇨Get Info. In the Info window, click the check box in the lower-left corner labeled Locked. A check in this box means that the file is locked and that you'll have to take an extra step to throw it out. To finish locking the file, click the close box in the upper-left corner of the Info window.

When a locked file is in the Trash, the only extra step required to delete the locked file is to hold down the Option key when choosing Special⇨Empty Trash. When you try to empty the Trash the normal way, you'll get a reminder that the Trash contains a locked file, and that file won't be deleted.

TIP: You can unlock a file by clearing (deselecting) the Locked check box in the file's Get Info window and then closing the window.

Making an alias of a file

An alias for a file gets around the rule that you can't be in two places at once. You create an alias for a file when you want two or more icons for the same file. The file can be a document, a program, or anything else on your Macintosh. What you do to the alias is actually done to the original. For example, double-clicking the alias opens the original file. Generally, you use an alias when you want to leave the original in one location and move the alias to a more convenient location. You can always recognize an alias by the fact that the name is shown in italics.

It's actually quite simple to make an alias. Simply click the file you want to use as the original and choose File⇨Make Alias (or press ⌘-M). The alias appears on top of the original and slightly offset. The name of the alias is the name of the original with the word *alias* added at the end. You can now move the alias to where you want it and, if you wish, change its name. Most of the time, you'll just want to remove the word *alias* from the end of the name.

TIP: To find the original of an alias, select the alias and then choose the File⇨Get Info command (or press ⌘-I). Then click the Find Original button to open the window containing the original file.

WARNING!: If you throw out the original file, the alias is useless. Unfortunately, there's no automatic way to get rid of all of the aliases when you throw out an original. You can, however, use File⇨Find to locate them. Throwing out the alias, on the other hand, doesn't affect the original at all.

Moving a file

You generally move a file from one place to another to improve the organization of your filing system. You will often move files into folders, but you can also move files to the desktop itself if that's where you want to store them.

To move a single file, you first need to pick it up: point to its icon with the cursor, press the button to select it, and hold down the button so that you are dragging the file. Drag the icon to the new location and release the button to drop the file into place.

If you're moving the file to a window, the inside border of the window darkens to show where you are placing the file. If you move onto a folder, the folder darkens. Releasing the mouse button while over a folder places the file into the folder. Finally, you can just drag the file over the desktop and release it to put it onto the desktop. Be aware that files on the desktop are actually stored on your disk in an invisible folder called the Desktop folder.

NOTE You need to arrange things before you start moving your files around. You want to be able to see where the file is starting from and where it's going. You need to be able to see the actual icon or name representing the file to pick it up, and you need to see either the part of the window where the file is to go or an icon representing the folder or disk where you want the file to end up.

NOTE When you place a file into a new window, the file is displayed using whatever view is being used for that window, which means that if you move an icon into a window in a list view, the file will be added to the list.

If you move a file to another disk, your Mac copies the file to the other disk. If you want, you can go back and throw out the original, but it doesn't really hurt to have a second copy as a backup.

If you've started moving a file and realize that you aren't sure where you want to put it, you can either drag it back to where you started or move it up onto the menu bar (where it says File, Edit, View and so on) and release the mouse button. When you try to place an icon on the menu bar, your Mac knows that you must be kidding and puts it back where it came from.

REFERENCE To find out about moving files that are part of a list within a window, see "Moving an item around on the list" in "List Things."

Moving a file (or alias) to the Apple menu

You put a file on the Apple menu for easy access no matter what program or window you're working in.

You should always use an alias of the file when you add it to the Apple menu. That way you can keep the original file neatly organized within the folder where it belongs.

REFERENCE If you don't know how to make an alias of a file, see the entry "Making an alias of a file" in this section or File⇨Make Alias in Part 2.

The easiest way to place an alias of a file on the Apple menu is to select the file by clicking it once. Then choose Apple menu⇨Automated Tasks⇨Add Alias to Apple Menu. That's it. Your Mac goes through all of the steps of making an alias and moving it where it belongs so that it appears on your Apple menu.

If you want to move an alias to the Apple menu the old-fashioned way (that is, without using the script in the Automated Tasks folder), it's really not all that hard. First make an alias of the file. (See "Making an alias of a file" if you don't know how.) Then move the alias to the Apple Menu Items folder, which is in the System Folder, which you'll find if you double-click your hard disk's icon.

Once a file, alias, or folder is in the Apple Menu Items folder, that item will appear in the Apple Menu.

a group of files

Before you can move a group of files, you have to select the group of files, and there are two ways to do this. The first is to click one icon and hold down the Shift key while you click each additional icon you want to add to the group. If you want to remove a file from the group, just make sure that you're still holding down the Shift key while you click the icon you want to remove.

The second method for selecting a group is to draw a *selection marquee* around them. You create a selection marquee by first clicking on the background of a window (not on any of the icons). Then hold down the mouse button and drag to enclose your selection. When you drag, you will see a rectangular border with one corner where you started and another at the pointer. As the border moves over part of an icon (or part of the icon's name), the icon is added to the group. When you release the button, anything touched by the rectangle or completely surrounded by the rectangle will be selected. You can now use the first method (Shift-clicking) to add or remove additional files to the selected group.

When you're ready to move the group of selected icons, put the arrow cursor over one of the selected icons, press and hold down the mouse button, and drag the group to its new location.

To stop moving a group of files, simply move the cursor up to the menu bar (where it says File, Edit, View and so on) and let go of the button. The files will be returned to where you started from.

Opening a file

The easiest way to open a file is to put your cursor over the file and double-click. The file will probably open right up so that you can use it.

If the file doesn't open, you'll get one of two messages.

- The best is a dialog box that tells you that your Macintosh "Could not find the application program" and a whole bunch of other text. The bottom line is that dialog box provides a list of programs, some of which may open the file. If you don't have a clue as to which one is the right choice, start at the top and work your way down. Either that or buy a box of Twinkies and go find your local guru.
- The other, less appealing dialog box tells you that your Macintosh just can't figure out what's going on. This one usually says something like "Application that created this file couldn't be found." There's only one thing to do — scream for help. If you're too shy for screaming, you might try opening a program that you suspect is capable of opening the file. With that program up and running, try to open the file using the program's Open command.

For some other methods for opening files, and a bit more on how System 7.5 recognizes files, see File⇨Open.

Printing a file

As with so many things on the Macintosh, there are two ways to print a file. The first is to click once on the file to select it and then choose File⇨Print. You're rewarded with the Print dialog box where you can specify some options and send your work off to the printer.

The other method requires a desktop printer — not the one on your physical desktop, but one on your Macintosh desktop that you can create using QuickDraw GX. First, you have to find the icon representing a printer. It probably looks a little bit like your real printer. (If you can't find one, you may need to create one. See Part 7 for all the details.) Once you've found the printer, put your cursor over the file you want to print, hold down the button, and drag the file on top of the printer icon. When you release the button, the file will be added to the printer queue (a waiting line for documents) and will print as soon as the printer is available.

See Part 7, "Printing Perfection," for all of the details and advice you'll need for printing.

Removing a file from the Apple menu

If you've added a number of files to the Apple menu, you'll find that it gets too crowded to be of any use. When that happens, it's time to take a few of the things off. Either get rid of the ones you hardly ever use, or consider putting some of the items directly onto the desktop.

Double-click your hard disk icon in the upper-right corner of the desktop and, in the window that appears, look for the System Folder (it has a little Macintosh on it). Double-click the System Folder and, in the window that opens, look for the Apple Menu Items folder (it has an Apple on it). When you find that folder, double-click on it. The window that opens contains one icon for each of the items on the Apple menu. Find the one you want to remove and drag it out of the window. (Put the arrow cursor over the icon, hold down the mouse button, drag the file so that it's outside the border of the window, and release the mouse button.) That's all that you need to do to get a file off the Apple menu.

Now, you need to decide what to do with the file. If it's an alias (the name is in italics), just trash it. Aliases are easy to make and you don't hurt the original file by throwing out an alias. If the file is an original, it may be your only copy. You should think about whether or not you want to keep it. If you don't, and you're absolutely sure you don't, go ahead and throw it away. Otherwise, move it to one of your folders for safekeeping.

Folder Things

A Folder

Most of the things that can be done to a file can also be done to a folder. A folder icon looks, well, like a folder, as the one to the left of this paragraph illustrates. You use folders to hold files as well as other folders. When you open a folder, you see its contents; when you move (or copy) a folder, all of its contents are also moved (or copied).

To move, copy, print or open a single file or group of files within a folder, see "File Things." To arrange the icons representing files and folders within a window, see "Icon Things." To organize and display a list of files and folders, see "List Things."

Changing a folder's name

You need to change a folder name when you realize that it should read "Macintosh Docs" rather than "McIntosh Docs" (unless you're writing about apples instead of computers).

The first step is to select the folder's name and only the name. Unfortunately, this is a pretty big first step. It's too easy to select the file rather than the name. To get the name, click once over the file name and then leave your cursor in the same position. After a moment, the background of the name should change from black to your highlight color. That's your signal that you're ready to edit the name. (You can also just click once and press Return, but it's often easier to wait.)

There are three basic editing techniques. The least sophisticated, but easiest, is to press the Delete key and just type the new name. The second is to highlight what you want to change and type in the new information. The final method is to click once where you want to insert characters (just start typing after the background turns white). You can also click to the right of characters you want to remove and use the Delete key to get rid of characters to the left of where you are.

There are some folder and volume names that you just can't change no matter how hard you try. Examples include your mailbox, a CD, and any files or folders on a CD.

Creating a new folder

Although most programs come already complete with their own folders for organizing their files, if you want to organize your own document files, you'll need to create your own folders. It's pretty straightforward and only takes a second.

If you're working with a bunch of icons, the first thing to do is make sure that the current active window is where you want the new folder to appear. If you're working with a window full of icons, the new folder is added in among the other icons. If you're working with a list view, it's a little more complicated. Because a single list view can show several levels of folders, you need to make sure that you have something selected within the same folder as where you want the new folder, and that what you've selected is at same level as where you want to add the new folder. (For more on levels of folders within list views, see "Expanding and collapsing the view of a folder" in "List Things.")

After you've decided where you want the new folder, choose File⇨New Folder. Somewhere on your screen, your Mac created a new, empty folder. Before you do anything else, before you click anywhere on the screen or press another key, think of what name you want to give this folder. Got it? Good. Now type that name. The reason for providing a name right away is that when a folder is first created, it's called "untitled folder." Not very informative. For your convenience, the name is already highlighted so that you can replace it by typing the new name. Immediately naming your folders is a very good habit to get into.

NOTE: If you are viewing the contents of the window as a list, when you change the name of the folder, its position on the list will probably also change.

TIP: You aren't restricted to letters or numbers in a Macintosh file name. You can use pretty much anything you can type — with the notable exception of the colon (:). Names that start with spaces will appear at the top of the list. Names that start with most other symbols, including the bullet you create by holding down the Option key and pressing 8, go to the end of the list.

Deleting a folder

Be very, very careful when you get rid of a folder. Throwing out the folder throws out all of the contents, so you need to be sure that there's nothing in there that you really needed. Deleting something from your Macintosh is a two-step process in part to make sure that you don't lose things by accident.

First, place the folder in the Trash (located in the lower-right corner of your desktop). To move a folder to the Trash, put your cursor over the folder, hold down the mouse button, and drag the cursor over the Trash. When the Trash darkens, it means you're in the right place and can go ahead and release the button. If the Trash was empty before you started, it's sides will bulge to show you that it contains something. If there's something else already in the Trash, you can add more things, but the sides won't get any bigger.

Just like in real life, you can dig through the Trash to retrieve a folder. To open the Trash, double-click it. You can open any of the folders within the Trash by double-clicking them. To salvage something from the Trash, simply drag it out of the Trash window (onto the desktop, onto a disk or folder, or into another window).

If you are sure that you don't want or need the contents of the Trash, you can empty the Trash by choosing Special⇨Empty Trash. A dialog box appears telling you how many items are in the Trash (including their total size). This is your last chance to change your mind. If you're still sure you want to delete what's in the Trash, click OK.

Sometimes, your Macintosh will refuse to do your bidding. This is particularly likely to happen with a full moon or when the Trash contains files that are locked or otherwise protected. If you get a message saying that the files cannot be thrown out, try holding down the Option key while you choose Special⇨Empty Trash.

Moving a folder (or an alias of a folder) onto the Apple menu

You put a folder (or an alias of a folder) on the Apple menu for easy access to its contents.

You should always use an alias of the folder when you add it to the Apple menu. To make an alias of a folder, click it once to select it and then choose File⇨Make Alias.

The easiest way to place an alias of a folder on the Apple menu is to select the folder by clicking it. Then choose Apple menu⇨Automated Tasks⇨Add Alias to Apple Menu. That's all there is to it. An alias of the folder now appears in the Apple menu.

If you want to move an alias of a folder to the Apple menu the old-fashioned way (that is, without using the script in the Automated Tasks folder), it's really not all that hard. Click the folder to select it. Choose File⇨Make Alias. An alias of the folder appears. Change the name of the alias if you wish. (See "Changing a folder's name" for all the details). Finally, move the alias to the Apple Menu Items folder, which is in the System Folder, which is on your hard disk's root level. The folder alias will now appear in the Apple menu.

If you need more details on making an alias, see "Making an alias of a file" in the "File Things" section. The same information applies to folders.

Moving or copying a folder

You generally move or copy a folder to improve the organization of your filing system. All of the techniques for moving or copying a file also work with a folder.

To move a single folder, you first need to pick it up — point to its icon with the arrow cursor, press the button to select it, and hold down the button so that you are dragging the folder with your cursor (move the mouse to move the folder). Move the folder to the new location and release the button to drop it into place. Most of the time, you'll hear these steps referred to as "drag it to a new location."

To put a folder inside of a second folder, drag the folder you want to move so that your cursor is on top of the second folder. When you are in the right spot, the second folder darkens and the background behind its name turns black. Release the mouse button and the folder you were dragging (and all of its contents) is inserted inside of the second.

To copy a folder within the same folder, select the folder by clicking on it once and then choose File⇨Duplicate. The new folder will have the word "copy" at the end, but the names of all of the items within the original folder and the copy will remain the same.

To copy a folder to a different location, hold down the Option while dragging the folder. If the Option key is held down when you release the mouse button, you'll copy the folder instead of moving it.

When you drag a folder onto another disk, you automatically make a copy of it.

TIP

You can move or copy a group of folders or a combination of folders and files if you first select the group. To select a group, click the first file or folder and then hold down the Shift key and click additional icons to add them to the group.

You can also create a *selection marquee* around the group. To draw a selection marquee, press and hold down the mouse button and drag from the upper left of any group of files or folders to the lower right. Make sure that you begin dragging on the window's background and not on any of the files or folders. As you move the mouse, you'll draw a rectangle. Any file or folder that is touched or enclosed by the rectangle will be selected.

TIP

File⇨Duplicate has a shortcut — ⌘-D. Just select the file, hold down the ⌘ key and press the letter D.

NOTE

To cancel copying or moving a folder, drag it up to the menu bar or back to where you started from.

Opening a folder

You open a folder to see what's inside of it. Unless you have x-ray vision, this is pretty much your only choice if you are working in an icon view. If you are working with information organized as a list, see the "List Things" section.

The easiest way to open a folder is to put your cursor over the file and double-click. The folder opens to reveal its contents in its own window.

Now that you have the folder's contents in a window, you may need to move the window. If so, see "Window Things."

Icon Things

Pretty much everything on your Macintosh can be represented as an icon. Along the left side of the screen are probably several icons representing your various disks with different icons for the different types of disks. When you open one of the disks, you'll see icons representing files and folders. Except for their color, almost all of folder icons look the same, but icons for programs and documents can come in many shapes and styles.

This section talks about controlling the way your window displays various icons. The "File Things" section covers how to work with those icons that represent files. The "Folder Things" section deals with doing things with folder icons. If you need info on viewing icons within lists, see the "List Things" section.

Lining up those icons

Depending upon your personality, it may be very important to you for your icons to line up neatly. In that case, you ought to read this section carefully. On the other hand, you may not care until you need to frantically try to straighten things out to find the one icon you need at the last moment. (Yes, I am a Virgo and do love organized lists and neat icons.)

To organize your icons, you need to use a menu command — Special⇨Clean Up Window. Be careful to check what the command says because it changes depending upon what you have selected and what keys you hold down. If you just go up to the Special menu and select the Clean Up Window command, all of the icons within the window are arranged into neat rows and columns. Icons already showing within the window that are already on your Macintosh's idea of rows or columns (called the *grid*) are not moved. Depending upon the setting for the grid in the Views control panel, you may have equally-spaced rows (called a straight grid) or staggered rows (using a staggered grid). The following figure shows two windows — one with a straight grid and one with a staggered grid. (If the first command on the Special menu says something other than Clean Up Window, read on for an explanation.)

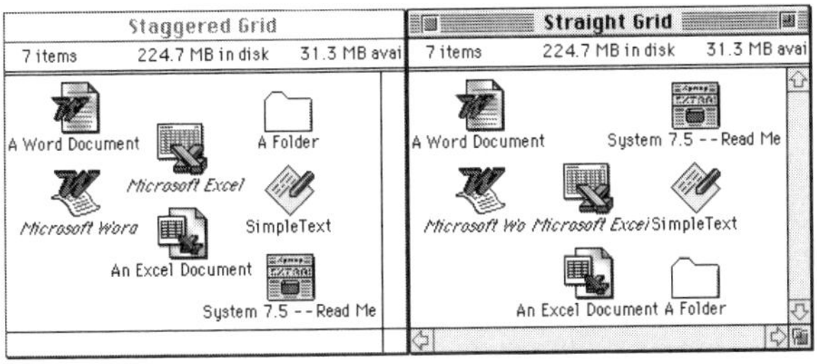

If you select just some of the icons within the window, you can hold down the Shift key while selecting the command to arrange just those icons. The menu command is Special⇨Clean Up Selection when the Shift key is down. There are a couple of ways to select a group of icons. The first method is to click one of the icons to get started and then hold down the Shift key while you click on other icons to add to the group. The second method is to drag a selection marquee around the icons by clicking on the window background to the upper left of the group, holding down the mouse button, and moving to the lower right of the group. Any icon that is enclosed or touched by the marquee will be selected. You can remove an icon from a group by holding down the Shift key and clicking the icon.

If you hold down the Option key when pulling down the Special menu, you get a command based upon what you last did in the List View. If you haven't ever used one of the List Views or you haven't made any changes to the order of the list, the command is Clean Up by Name. Otherwise, the command uses whatever choice you made when you were viewing the list — Clean Up by Kind, Clean Up by Size, Clean Up by Date, and so on. If you select Clean Up by Name, the icons are sorted alphabetically by name from left to right and top to bottom. Clean Up by Kind groups similar kinds of documents; Clean Up by Size puts things in order from largest to smallest; Clean Up by Date puts the most recent files first, and so on.

For those of us who believe that organization should be a way of life, Apple has thoughtfully provided the Views control panel, which has an option that forces icons to snap to the proper position. You'll never have to line them by hand again. By the way, if you don't have a window open, the Clean Up command with nothing selected is Clean Up Desktop; it's discussed under Desktop Things. The Clean Up All command and a bit more detail on each of the other Clean Up commands is included under Special⇨Clean Up in Part 2.

Printing a picture of the window's contents

If you want a record of all of the icons that are within the window, you can print a copy of the window's contents. This feature is useful for recording the contents of folders or disks.

All you need to do is select the window you want to print and choose File⇨Print Window and click OK in the resulting Print dialog box.

While there's nothing wrong with printing a picture of a bunch of icons, it's usually more helpful to have a list of the files. In other words, you should be in a list view rather than an icon view when you print a window. For information on list views, see the entries under "List Things."

Viewing icons

System 7.5 allows you to view the contents of windows in several different ways. You access many of the various viewing options in, you guessed it, the View menu in the Finder.

When using the View menu, you need to decide if you want big icons or little icons. With little icons, you can fit more of them in a window. With big icons, you can actually see what they are. I have a bit of a bias towards the ones I can see.

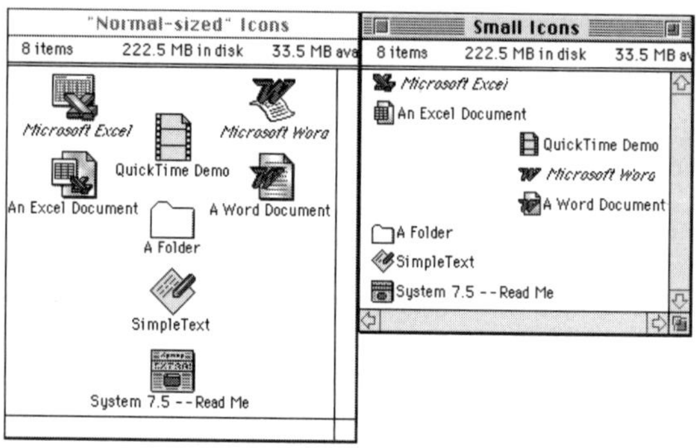

To change the icon view for a window, first select that window by clicking within it. Pull down the View menu and choose either by Icon (for the larger size) or by Small Icon. Your window immediately changes to the view you requested.

Any changes you make in one icon view are reflected in the other. The problem is that you may position things so that they're readable with small icons and then find that when you switch to the regular icon view, your icon names overlap and you can't see some of the icons in the window. There's nothing you can really do about it, except reorganize the icons, but it's good to know.

You can only change the view for the active window (the one you are currently working in).

The View menu contains several other viewing options (by Name, by Size, and so on). These options (the List views) are covered under "List Things." You can find out about changing the size, shape, or position of windows in "Windows Things."

List Things

The list views enable you to see an overview of the contents of one or more folders. Each of the list views (accessed via the Views menu) lets you see the contents of the current folder or disk sorted by one of seven categories. All of them also let you see the contents of any of the folders within the current folder, and any folder within those folders, all the way down to the very last folder within a folder. The ways in which folders are displayed in a list are described in "Expanding the list for a folder" a little later in this section.

If you'd rather work with icons (which seems somewhat easier when you're dealing with just the items in the current folder), you should look at "Icon Things" for an overview of viewing icons.

Changing the categories displayed in a list

There's one big problem with viewing a list of icons: if you try to show all of the possible categories, they won't fit across your screen. Now, this could mean you need to buy a bigger screen, but it's probably easier (and certainly cheaper) to just change which categories are shown.

List categories are controlled by the Views control panel. To access it, choose Apple menu⇨Control Panels⇨Views. The bottom half of the Views control panel, section called List Views, is shown here.

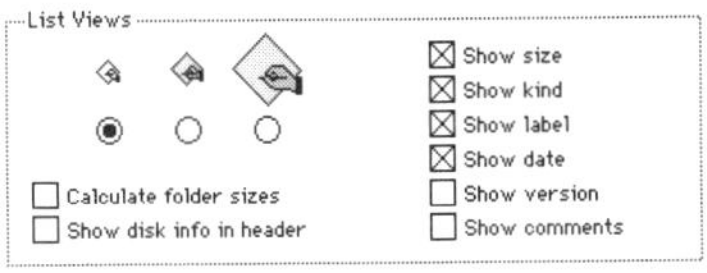

Notice over on the right is a series of check boxes that all start with the word *Show*. Well, these control what will, you guessed it, show in the list views. They also control which options appear in the View menu. For example, if the Show date option is checked, the date is displayed in the list view and the by Date command appears in the View menu.

Put your mouse over the check box next to the item you want to add or remove and click the mouse button. When you click, checked boxes clear and cleared boxes get a check. It's what the nerds call a *toggle*. A toggle, such as a check box, has two settings that you can flip between — on and off. When you have checked the categories that you want to have appear, close the Views control panel by clicking its close box in the upper-left corner.

You've done it! Your list categories have been changed.

Expanding and collapsing the view of a folder

The most significant advantage of working with one of the list views is that you can compare what is in two different folders and even, should the mood strike you, move items between the folders on your list. The key to this technology is the capability to expand and collapse the various levels of your list.

In a list view, each folder has a small triangle to the left of it. If the triangle seems to be pointing to the right, then the folder is *closed* — you aren't viewing it's contents. If the folder seems to be pointing downward, then the folder is *opened* and you can see what's inside. Critics may point out that each triangle has three corners and can point in three directions at once. Critics are a real problem for authors, but I'll ignore them for the moment.

Folders that are on the top level of the window are shown all the way to the left of the window. Folders within those folders are indented about a quarter of an inch. Each additional level of folders within folders goes another quarter inch to the right. The folders that are to the far left are referred to as being at the top-most level of the window and are the only ones you would see if you were using an icon view. The following figure shows the little triangles and the indented levels of folders.

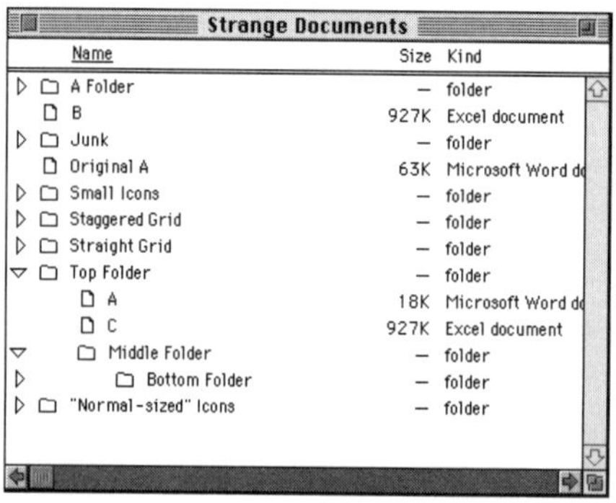

Now, those little triangles over on the left are very important. You use them to expand or collapse the view into a folder. Click on the triangle and it rotates, switching between pointing down (the folder is expanded and you can see the contents) and pointing right (the folder is collapsed).

For those of you who prefer using the keyboard, and you know who you are, there are keyboard commands for expanding and collapsing. Use the up arrow and down arrow on your keyboard to move through the list. When you have a folder name highlighted, you can hold down the ⌘ key and use the left arrow to expand the folder or ⌘ with the right arrow to collapse it.

Expanding and collapsing all the levels of a folder

Often, you want to see everything that's hiding within a folder, no matter how deeply buried. You may be reorganizing your entire filing system and want to get an overview, or you might be looking at someone else's system trying to figure out where that person stored the copy of the report that's due in an hour.

For a picture of the list view and the triangles that control whether a folder is open or closed, see "Expanding and collapsing the view of a folder," which is the entry just before this one.

To see all of the levels of folders within a folder, hold down the Option key while you expand the top-most folder. You can either hold down Option and click on the triangle to the left of the folder's name or select the folder's name and hold down both the Option key and the ⌘ key and press the right arrow. Either works. Both are fairly easy.

When it comes time to collapse a folder, you won't see any immediate difference between collapsing the top-most level or the entire collection of subfolders. In either case, what you end up with is a closed folder. The difference comes when you open that folder again. If you just collapsed the top-most folder by clicking on its triangle or pressing ⌘-left arrow, when you open the folder again, the folders within will be the same as when you last looked into the folder. If every folder was expanded, then they'll all be expanded when you reopen the folder. If some were closed and some were open, they'll be exactly the same. On the other hand, if you hold down the Option key while closing the folder, when you open the folder again, all of the folders within will be closed. To close all of the levels of folders within a folder, you can either hold down the Option key and click the triangle or hold down both the Option key and the ⌘ key and press the left arrow.

Listing what's in the window

You use the View menu to change the way a list is organized within a window. The list views are the ones that begin with *by*, as in by Name, by Size, and so on. The one choice that's always available is View⇨by Name, so maybe it's the one you should memorize. Other list view options are available depending on the settings in the Views control panel. The other list views include by Size, by Comments, by Kind, by Date, by Version, and by Label.

To display the contents of the active window as a list sorted by name, choose View⇨by Name. That's all there is to it. Only the view in the active window changes, so make sure that you select the window you want to work with before choosing a list view.

TIP: To get an overview of how your hard disk is organized, double-click its icon to show the top-most level of the disk. Then change to a list view and you'll be able to see into any folder anywhere on that disk.

REFERENCE: You can easily change which category is used to sort the items on the list. To find out how, see "Sorting the list on one of the columns." To change which information about each file is included in the list, see "Changing the categories displayed in a list." Both entries are in this section.

Moving an item around on the list

A list view makes it easier to reorganize your files and folders. With the capability to open and view the contents of several folders within a single window, you will often use a list view to move files and folders among other folders.

Put your cursor over the item you want to move, press and hold down the mouse button, and drag the item to any of the folders showing on the list. As you move the item over a folder, its name highlights, which indicates that if you release the mouse button, the item will be placed in that folder. When you have the item where you want it, release the mouse button.

Of course, you need to be able to see the folder where you want to put the item. Often, this means that you should expand any folders that you want to work with, but don't worry if the entire list doesn't fit into the window. When you are holding down the mouse button to move an item, reaching the top or bottom of the window causes the list to move as though you were using the scroll bars. Just drag the icon right over the border and the list will start to move.

TIP: If you want to move something to the top-most level in the window, there doesn't appear to be anywhere to put it. If you put your cursor on top of a folder, whatever you're moving ends up in that folder. If there are other types of icons at the top-most level, you can move the item on top of any of those icons and the item will move to the top level of the folder. But what if all you have at the top-most level are folders? Don't despair, there is a solution. Move the item up to where the names of the categories appear (just below the title bar). When you release the mouse button, the item or items you're moving will be placed at the top-most level.

NOTE

You can move several items at once. The easiest way to do this is by moving an entire folder. Any time that you move a folder, all of its contents move with it.

A second approach is to move a group of individual items. To select a group, click on the first one and then hold down the Shift key and click on other items to add them to the group. When you move individual items as a group, all of the individual selected items will be placed at the same level within the folder you choose to put them in.

If you want to select several items that are together on the list, you can use a selection marquee to select them. Point just to the left of the first item you want to select, hold down the mouse button, move to the right until the first name is selected, and then, with the mouse button still down, move to the last item you want to select. This action should select all of the items between the first and the last.

If you need to remove an item from a selected group, hold down the Shift key and click it.

NOTE

When creating new folders within a list, you need to select something at the proper level. If you want to create a folder at the top-most level, just select anything at that level (a file icon or a folder that's aligned at the far left) and then choose File⇨New Folder. To create a folder within another folder, first expand the folder that you want to contain the new folder and then select something within the folder. Now, when you choose File⇨New Folder, the new folder will appear within the other one.

Opening a file or folder from list view

It would be pretty silly if you had to return to an icon view in order to open a file or a folder in a separate window. Fortunately, that's not the case. With list view, you can display the contents of a folder without opening it as a separate window, but it's often convenient to be able to display the contents of two different folders side-by-side.

To open either a file or a folder in the list view, double-click anywhere on the line for that item except for the little triangle on the far left. The little triangle is used to open and close folders within the list view. To learn how to use it, see "Expanding and collapsing the view of a folder" earlier in this section.

Actually, any of the techniques for opening a file work in list views. You can use File⇨Open, ⌘-O, or ⌘-down arrow.

All of the basic things you might want to do to a file or group of files work the same whether you are using a list or icon view. The one thing that's a bit different (and, in fact, even easier) is moving files between the folders on your list. See the entry "Moving an item around on the list" for more info.

Printing a list of the window's contents

There are times when you just need the feel of paper in your hand. You may be trying to come up with a scheme to organize all of your files or you might just need a list of everything that's on a particular disk. The easiest way to get a listing of your file's names onto paper is to print the list view of a window.

First, make sure that the window is listing everything that you want on the paper. Then choose File⇨Print Window. In the resulting dialog box, click the Print button or press return to get things going. After that, you can just sit back and watch your list print away.

Only the things that are showing in the list are printed, so you should expand and collapse folders as needed to get exactly what you want to print. Don't worry about whether the list fits into the window, though, because the entire list is printed no matter how long it is.

Sorting the list on one of the columns

Let's face it. The usual reason for using list views is to help you find the files that you created and now can't find. One technique for looking for something within a window is to sort the list of the window's contents by different categories. For example, if you're looking for a file that you worked on last week, you can sort the list by Date and all of last week's files will be grouped together.

When you're looking at a list of files in a folder, changing the category used for sorting is pretty easy. Just click on the column heading you want to sort by. That's it. You're done. Now, wasn't that easy. Don't you wish you could organize your real filing cabinet that fast.

Every folder shown in the list within a single window is sorted using the same category. If you want to compare two folders using different categories to sort them, you'll need to open two different windows — one for each folder.

The category you use to sort your list is also available for sorting your icons. Just change to an icon view and hold down the Option key while choosing Special⇨Clean Up by *???*. The *???* is replaced with whatever category you sorted by (Clean Up by Name, Clean Up by Date, Clean Up by Kind and so on).

Of course, if you've really lost a file, your best bet is to use File⇨Find. It's described in Part 2.

Window Things

A window gives you a view into something — generally a disk, a folder or a document. Some of the previous sections cover how to deal with the things inside of windows. This section deals with things you can do to the window itself. You open a window by opening the thing you want to look into. So, for example, to open a window to view what's inside a folder, you open the folder.

Although you can have as many windows open as you want, only one of them can be active. The active window is the one with lines in its title bar (up where the name is) and appears to be on top of the other windows. In the following figure, the window on the left is the active one.

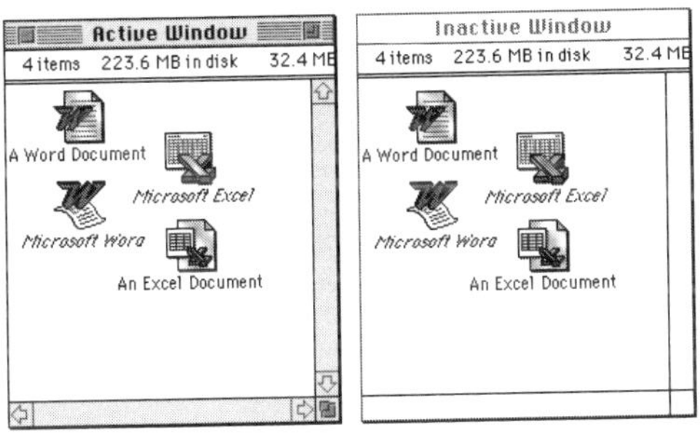

Most often, you'll be working with your windows in order to see the contents of several at once. For example, you may need to arrange two windows so that you can see the file you want to move in one window and the folder where you want to put it in another. You need to know how to move, size, close, and roll up windows.

See "Icon Things" and "List Things" for details on controlling how things in a window are organized. To actually work with the things you see inside of the window, see "File Things" and "Folder Things." Opening folders is covered in "Folder Things," and opening disks is covered in "Disk Things."

Changing the size of a window

There are a number of reasons why you might change the size of a window, but the most common is that you are trying to fit several windows on your screen at one time. It's much easier to learn this skill than it is to find the money to buy a larger monitor.

Down in the lower-right corner of almost every window is the *size box*. It's a little square on top of and a bit offset from a bigger square. If that description doesn't give you a brilliant visual image, here's a picture of a size box.

Put the cursor over the size box and press and hold down the mouse button. You should see a dotted outline around the window's borders. When you move the mouse, the right side and the bottom of the outline move along with the mouse. Move the border's outline to the size you want and then release the mouse button. The window changes shape to match the outline.

There's no way to change the size of a window using the top or left side, but you can get the same effect by making the window the size you want and then moving it to where you want it.

You will often have to put the cursor inside the size, close, or zoom box of a window, so it's important to know that the *hot spot* of the cursor is the very point of the arrow. The hot spot is where your Macintosh thinks the cursor really is. All you need to do is make sure that the point is in the box — the rest of the arrow can be hanging out over the edge.

Some windows don't have a size box at all. Try putting the mouse over the lower-right corner and dragging anyway. Often, you will be able to resize the window even though a size box isn't showing. If this technique doesn't work, you're probably out of luck. Fortunately, you can change the size of almost all windows you encounter in the Finder and document windows you work with when using programs.

Closing all windows

If your desktop is just too cluttered with opened windows, it may be time to close them all and start over. Fortunately, there's a simple trick that lets you sit back and watch your windows close themselves, one by one.

Hold down the Option key while you close a window. You can either hold down Option while you click in the close box (in the upper-left corner of the window's title bar) or hold down the Option key and choose File⇨Close Window.

Closing a window

At some point in your Macintosh adventure, you'll decide that you have too many windows open on your desktop. No matter how small you make them, they still get in the way. Now it's time to start closing a few of them.

You may have noticed that three out of the four corners of a window have little boxes. The one up there in the left corner is the *close box.* One simple click with the cursor inside the close box and the window closes.

Whenever you have to put the cursor inside one of those little boxes, it's important to know that the *hot spot* of the cursor is the very point of the arrow. The hot spot is where your Mac thinks the cursor really is. All you need to do is make sure that the point is in the close box — the rest of the arrow can be hanging out over the edge.

If you have a window that you use often and don't want to close it (because it takes too long to open), you can reduce it down to the size of the its title bar. See the entry "Rolling up the window shade" (covered later in this section).

Closing a window automatically

When you go to open a program or document, it's often nice if your Macintosh cleans up behind you. One of the ways you can do this is by automatically closing your current window when you open a new one. It doesn't matter whether your new window is another folder, a different disk, or a document within an application. This trick will work for all of them.

Hold down the Option key while opening your new window. You can either hold down the Option key and double-click what it is you're opening or hold down Option and choose File⇨Open. Both work just fine.

Listing the folders back to the desktop

Sometimes you may lose track of where you are within your folders. It's useful to know the path back up to the desktop level. Nerds always talk about the *path* as being from the desktop to the current file or folder, but we're a bit more flexible and can go in either direction along the path.

To see a list of the folders in the path back to the desktop, position the cursor above the name showing in the title bar of the current window, press and hold the ⌘ key, and press and hold the mouse button. You'll get a list like the one shown in the following figure.

If you want to move to one the folders in the list, keep the mouse button down and move the cursor so that it highlights the desired folder name. When you release the mouse button, the window for that folder opens.

Making a window active

You need to make a window active in order to use any of the things inside of the window. You don't need to make the window active if it's where you are going to put something. In other words, you can move something from the active window to an inactive window without having to worry about making the second window active.

Making a window active is probably the easiest thing you'll ever do on your Macintosh. Just click once on any part of the window that is visible.

NOTE

When you open a folder or a disk, the new window is automatically the active window.

If you click on a document window that is associated with a program that is open, you will move to that program. Sure, it makes the window active, but you also are no longer working with files, folders, and windows, but with your document instead.

REFERENCE

Of course, you may need to move another window in order to see part of the window that you want to make active. See either "Moving an active window" or "Moving an inactive window" in this section if you need help.

Making a window really big

For those occasions when you are focused on the contents of a single window and don't want to bother changing the size the slow way, use the zoom box. The zoom box is the fastest way to make a window as large as necessary or possible.

The zoom box is located in the upper-right corner of most windows and looks like a large square with a smaller square in its upper-left corner. For those of you who prefer a visual approach, see the figure on the left.

Click in the zoom box to make the window jump in size. The zoom box has two settings — big and little. If you click the zoom box and the window gets smaller, click it again to make it jump back to the large size.

Clicking the zoom box doesn't always make a window take up the full screen. It really zooms the window to the largest size or a size sufficient to show the entire contents of the window. Your Macintosh first tries to fit the window tightly around the contents. If it can, great. It stays with that size. If it can't, it keeps expanding until it's as large as possible and then stops. With list views, you often end up with a window that's as wide as the screen permits.

In the Finder, the zoom box will never expand a window so that it covers the disk icons and the Trash along the right side of the desktop. You can, however, manually enlarge a window to cover this portion of the desktop if you want. See "Changing the size of the window" for details.

Whenever you have to put the cursor inside of the zoom, size, or close box, it's important to know that the *hot spot* of the cursor is the very point of the arrow. The hot spot is where your Macintosh thinks the cursor really is. All you need to do is make sure that the point is in the box — the rest of the arrow can be hanging out over the edge.

Moving an active window

The most common time for wanting to move the active window is to get at something underneath. You need to do that if you are copying something from the active window and can't see where you want to put it.

The first thing you gotta do is find the title bar of the active window. It's at the top of the window, and its the place where the name of the window goes . Look, there's one now.

Point to the title bar anywhere except on those little boxes at either end and then press and hold down the mouse button. A dotted outline appears around the window. As you move the mouse, the window's outline follows the cursor. When you release the mouse button, the window jumps over and fills up the outline.

If a dialog box has a title bar, the odds are good that you can move it just like a window. It never hurts to try.

For more info on maneuvering in and around windows, see "Moving an inactive window" and "Changing the size of a window." Also check out "Rolling up the window shade" for the scoop on a cool new feature of System 7.5.

Moving an inactive window

You might move an inactive window so that you can see more of it or because it's covering up something else that you need to see. The technique detailed in this entry enables you to move a window in the background without making it active.

You need to find the title bar of the inactive window before you can move it. The title bar is where the name of the window appears; if it's inactive, it won't have anything else showing — no lines, no zoom box, no close box. If any of those things are showing, what you have is an active window.

Put the cursor over the title bar of the inactive window, hold down the ⌘ key, and press and hold down the mouse button. You should see a dotted outline around the window, and when you move the mouse, the outline follows the cursor. When you release the mouse button, the window moves to the position of the outline and remains inactive.

This trick doesn't work if the window is a document window from a program. When you click on a document window's title bar, that window becomes active.

Rolling up the window shade

If you want to move a window out of the way but know that you'll be using its contents later, you may just want to roll it up into the title bar. This is a neat trick that you can do on the desktop as well as within programs.

It's really quite simple. Double-click the title bar to roll up the window. Double-click the title bar to roll down the window shade. Double-click after double-click, it keeps rolling up and down.

Actually, double-clicking is just the standard option for controlling the window shade. You use the WindowShade control panel to choose between two or three clicks and to set whether you need to hold down the Command, Control, or Option key (or some combination) while clicking.

If you want to make the title bar smaller, you need to do that before rolling up the shade. See "Changing the size of a window" earlier in this section. Whether or not your windows have window shades and whether or not your shades make cool sounds while rolling up and down is controlled by the WindowShade control panel.

Part 2

Command Reference

?⇨About Apple Guide

NEW 7.5

Shows you a one-window guide to the basics of the Apple Guide system. It isn't a lot of information, but it's enough to get you started.

Just the facts

Choose ?⇨About Apple Guide to get less information than you can from this Quick Reference. Admittedly, Apple's information all fits on two screens, but it only gives you a brief description of each item on the ? menu and a much smaller sample window than the one you'll find in this Quick Reference under ?⇨Macintosh Guide. When you're done looking at the window, click in the close box in the upper-left corner to make it go away. For a description of the Guide screen, see ?⇨Macintosh Guide.

?⇨Hide Balloons

Stops the display of balloon help, which can considerably improve the performance of your Macintosh. This command is only available if you've already turned on balloon help.

Just the facts

Choose ?⇨Hide Balloons to turn off balloon help. As soon as balloon help is turned off, the command changes to ?⇨Show Balloons.

More Stuff

NOTE

There's really nothing more to be said, except that most people keep balloon help off until they really need it. It can be annoying at times.

?⇨Macintosh Guide

NEW 7.5

Answers any and all of your questions about using your Macintosh without you having to consult a book. Now, of course, if it worked, I wouldn't be happy because you wouldn't be reading this. Because you are, it's obvious that while the Macintosh Guide is useful, it's not the solution to all problems.

For keyboard krazies

⌘ + ?

Just the facts

Immediately after selecting ?⇨Macintosh Guide (or pressing ⌘-?), you'll get a message that says *One moment please*. Before too long, that message disappears and is replaced by the opening screen for the Macintosh guide. To use a guide, you need to know a few basic facts about the guide screen. The first step is to learn the various parts of the guide window (conveniently labeled in the following figure).

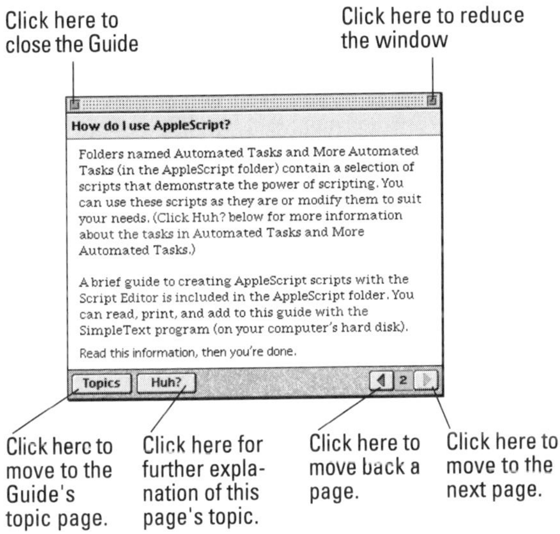

You use the arrows on the guide window to move around through the various topics. Notice that the title bar for the guide is different from that of a normal window. It indicates that you can move the guide window, but it always remains on the top of the desktop (covering up parts of any windows beneath it). You can, however, move the guide anywhere on your screen. Clicking in the zoom box closes the guide to a smaller window where just the title of the current topic is displayed.

There are three different ways to find something within the Macintosh Guide and, coincidentally, three buttons across the top of the dialog box. To look at the list of topics used within the Macintosh Guide, click the Topics button. The middle of the screen should now contain two list boxes. The one on the left contains the main topics in the guide. Scroll through the list until you find a topic that looks like the one you want and then click the topic. After you choose a topic in the list on the left, the list on the right shows a list of specific entries. To use one of the entries, simply double-click the entry for the help you need.

There are three main types of entries in a guide. The first are shown under the *How do I* heading. When you select one of these entries, the help that is displayed is designed to walk through a task on your Macintosh. This is probably one of the neatest features in System 7.5. If you can't figure out how to do something, you can get your Mac to do the work for you. In addition, your Mac uses a mark that resembles the one from bright red marking pen to show you where things are on your screen. In many cases, you can click the Huh? button for more help with what you're trying to do. The second type of entries, shown under *Definitions*, are much more boring. These topics are all single-pages, and they provide you with a definition of the selected term. The final type of entry is shown under one of two headings — *Why can't I* and just plain *Why*. These topics try to explain what problems might be occurring when your Macintosh refuses to cooperate and complete a task — especially when you're sure you followed all of the directions.

Back to the main screen and the other two ways of choosing topics within the Macintosh Guide. If you click the Index button, you get an alphabetical list of every topic within the guide. You can either scroll through the list or move the indicator at the top of the list so that it covers the letter you want to jump to. The third method is to click the Look For button to display a smaller box on the left to hold the words you want to search for (rather than a list). Click the button next to the box and enter a word or group of words that describe what you're looking for. Click the Search button and the guide either lists any topic with a title that contains all of the words that you enter or tells you which of your words it can't find. Sometimes the guide can find all of your words, but not in a single title. In that case, it tells you to try again with fewer words.

More Stuff

WARNING! You may find yourself staring more at the *One moment please* message than at any helpful information because your Macintosh displays this message every time you switch between major topics.

TIP The different guides are each organized slightly differently, but you can usually be sure that any buttons across the top are for choosing a method for finding a topic; any windows in the middle are used for choosing a particular topic.

NOTE

Apple Guide is a new technology introduced with System 7.5. It is intended to provide a standard method for presenting help information. In other words, Apple's idea is that the developers of the programs that you actually use on your Macintosh will adopt the guides for their help files. Only time will tell if this really happens. Right now, it seems like each of the different developers has a different help system for their programs.

?⇨PowerTalk Guide

NEW 7.5

A specialized guide for learning the new PowerTalk features.

Just the facts

REFERENCE

For more on using PowerTalk, see Part 8. To learn more about using guides, see ?⇨Macintosh Guide.

?⇨Shortcuts

Provides a guide with some of the most common and useful shortcuts for using your Macintosh. Almost all of the shortcuts listed here are well worth the time it takes to learn them.

Just the facts

After you choose ?⇨Shortcuts, you get a guide screen that shows you six buttons, each representing a different category of shortcuts. Click any of the buttons to move to a series of guide screens with more about the shortcuts in that category. You move between the various pages in each topic by clicking the left and right arrows in the lower-right corner of the screen. To return to the opening screen with its category buttons, click the up arrow in the lower-left corner of the screen. To close the guide, click in the close box in the upper-left corner.

More Stuff

TIP

There's another set of tips and shortcuts in the Macintosh Guide. To get to those, choose ?⇨Macintosh Guide and then click the Topics button. Scroll down in the list until you can see the last topic — Tips, Features, Other Information. Click the topic and then, when the list appears on the right, double-click Tips for efficient Macintosh use. This set of tips is more of a general guide on how to use your Macintosh rather than keyboard or mouse shortcuts, but it's useful nonetheless.

REFERENCE

The various parts of the guide window are shown with descriptive labels under ?⇨Macintosh Guide.

?⇨Show Balloons

Turns on balloon help, which causes little help balloons to appear next to the various menu commands and desktop icons. Not only is balloon help useful when working with System 7.5, but you'll find balloon help within many programs as well.

Just the facts

The first step is to choose ?⇨Show Balloons. This command turns the feature on, but to use it requires a second step. Put your cursor over whatever you need help with and wait a moment. A little balloon should appear with a brief description of whatever it is you're pointing at. If you need help with a menu item, pull down the menu and highlight the item. Keep holding the mouse button down until the balloon appears. If you decide that you don't want to use the command after all, move the cursor so that it's no longer over the menu before releasing the mouse button.

More Stuff

NOTE

The balloons aren't the kind that you fill with helium, but rather the kind they use in comics to show dialog. So far, balloon help is the only way your Macintosh talks to you about how to use it, but talking help screens with video can't be far behind.

Apple menu⇨About This Macintosh

Shows you what version of the System you are using (probably 7.5 to go with this Quick Reference), the total amount of working memory on your computer, the programs that are currently running, and the amount of memory used by each program. This is all very important information when you have a problem with one of your programs and need to ask your local guru for help.

Just the facts

A super-simple Macintosh command. Just go on up to that there Apple menu and choose About This Macintosh. The only problem is that unlike almost all of the other commands on the Apple menu, sometimes this one isn't where you left it. About This Macintosh is only available when you are working with the Finder.

More Stuff

NOTE

The About This Macintosh dialog box also tells you how much, if any, memory is being used as a RAM disk and, by subtracting the Built-In Memory from the Total Memory, how much disk space, if any, is being used as Virtual Memory. The creation of a RAM disk and the use of Virtual Memory are controlled by the Memory control panel and are really a bit beyond the scope of this book. But, you paid your money, so a quick explanation is in order. A RAM disk is a portion of working memory used as though it were disk storage. And because accessing RAM is much faster than reading or writing to a disk, a RAM disk is a very speedy, albeit temporary, form of storage. Virtual Memory is almost the opposite — it lets programs use disk storage as though it were working memory. This feature lets you run larger programs or more programs at one time. The down side to Virtual Memory is that it can significantly slow down your Mac.

CROSS-REFERENCE FOR DUMMIES

For more information about working with memory, see Chapter 10 of *Macintosh System 7.5 For Dummies*.

Apple menu⇨AppleCD Audio Player

Plays music using your Macintosh's CD-ROM drive and an audio CD. This is a nice feature for keeping you entertained while you work and might be the secret reason that so many people are buying CD-ROM drives.

Just the facts

You can either put the CD with the music into your disk drive and then choose Apple menu⇨AppleCD Audio Player or choose this desk accessory and then put the disk in. It doesn't really matter which you do first. After you've got a CD with music in the drive and have selected Apple menu⇨AppleCD Audio Player, you get a window that looks like the front of a car stereo floating on your screen. In fact, there's one floating on the next page right now. Use the controls in this window just as you would any stereo system. Go ahead. Have fun.

NOTE

It's no great shock that the sound quality from your Macintosh won't rival the most expensive stereo equipment. It is, however, better than most of the clock radios you find in most offices.

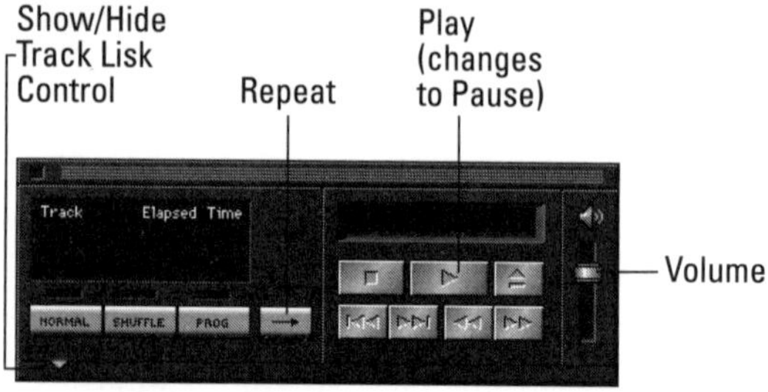

Unfortunately, some machines won't play audio CDs at all (especially if they don't have CD-ROM drives), and the sound quality varies depending on the kind of Mac you have and whether you're outputting to the internal speaker or external speakers.

Apple menu➪Automated Tasks

Performs a wide variety of very useful actions using the new System 7.5 scripting capabilities. Each of these scripts serves a different function. Automated Tasks is actually a folder residing somewhere on your Mac that contains a number of script files with an alias for the folder inside your Apple Menu Items folder (within your System Folder).

Just the facts

Selecting one of the script names causes your Macintosh to perform a recorded series of actions. For more information about scripts, see Part 6.

Apple menu➪Calculator

Adds, subtracts, multiplies and divides much faster than I can with or without using my fingers. In addition, you can copy the answer into whatever document you wish.

Just the facts

Right after you choose the Calculator from the Apple menu, a small calculator appears, floating in the middle of your screen. You can either use the mouse to click the keys on-screen, or you can use the keys on the numeric keypad to enter your calculation. Pressing your finger against the screen won't work.

Press the Clear key once (or click the C button once) to clear the current value from the Calculator and press it twice to clear out the entire calculation and start over.

More Stuff

The new, improved super-cool Graphing Calculator for Power Macs is discussed under Apple menu⇨Graphing Calculator.

Apple menu⇨Chooser

Determines which printers are installed on your desktop, establishes your network communications, and is just an all around nice command. Probably one of the most overworked commands on your Macintosh, but absolutely critical if you want to ever get anything out of the little box to share with other people.

Just the facts

Using Apple menu⇨Chooser to create a desktop printer is discussed along with the other printing commands in Part 7. Using Apple menu⇨Chooser with networking is covered in Part 8.

Apple menu⇨Control Panels

Opens the entire would of customization up for your delight. A control panel is a window in which you can specify various options for many of the features of your Macintosh. Among others, there are control panels for setting the pattern for the desktop background, controlling the volume and style of the system's beep, changing how quickly you have to double-click your mouse, and controlling your Macintosh's connection to a network.

Just the facts

The old-fashioned way of selecting a control panel is to simply choose the Control Panel folder from the Apple menu, find the icon for the control panel you want to use in the window that opens, and then double-click that icon.

NEW 7.5 The new and improved method of using a particular control panel requires that your Apple Menu Options control panel be set to show submenus. If it is, when you highlight Control Panels on the

Apple menu, a submenu appears to the right. This submenu lists all of the control panels currently within the Control Panels folder; you use the submenu to move directly to the control panel you need. After you've highlighted the Control Panels folder on the Apple menu, keep the mouse button down and slide the cursor over onto the submenu. You can now move the cursor up and down the submenu to choose the control panel you want. Choose the control panel from the submenu the same way you normally select a menu item — highlight it and then release the mouse button. The control panel you picked opens immediately for your customizing pleasure.

REFERENCE: Because each control panel works with a different aspect of your Macintosh, they are discussed individually in Part 4. The first entry, Apple Menu Options, covers how to turn the Apple menu submenus on and off.

Apple menu⇨Find File

NEW 7.5: Opens the Find dialog box for use in searching for files on your Macintosh. This is really the exact same command as the File⇨Find command, but it's easier to use because it's on the Apple menu, which means that you can use it without having to go back to the Finder.

Just the facts

REFERENCE: Fortunately, I wasn't so short of material that I had to describe this command twice. For an explanation, you need to turn to File⇨Find.

Apple menu⇨Graphing Calculator

POWER MAC: Creates two- and three-dimensional graphs based on the equations you enter. Not only is this great fun, but it will definitely improve your grade if you're ever forced to take trigonometry or calculus. It can also be used as a regular calculator with a lot more functions than the standard one on the Apple menu.

Just the facts

You open the Graphing Calculator by choosing Graphing Calculator from the Apple menu. (Tell me, were you surprised?) At the top of its window, you can enter the equation that you want to work with.

If you want to use the Graphing Calculator to do math, don't worry about entering any variables. Just enter the equation you want solved and then choose Equation⇨Evaluate. The portion of the equation you have selected is replaced with its result.

For more complex equations, you can select Equation⇨Show Full Keypad for a collection of common constants and mathematical operations to use in your equations. These include things like pi, raise 10 to the power of *x*, *x* squared, and the trigonometric functions. There are two special keys that you should be aware of. Clicking the Inverse key changes the buttons so that they represent all of the inverse functions. *X* squared becomes the square root of *x*; raise 10 to the power of *x* becomes the log of *x*, and so on. The Hyperbolic functions change the trigonometric functions so that they use the hyperbolic form. (Don't ask me to explain all of the details — I dropped my Physics major in college.)

If you want to create a graph, you can create a simple, two-dimensional graph by writing your equation with the variable *y* on the left of the equal sign and the equation in terms of *x* on the right. Actually, you can write an equation for *y* on the left and an equation for *x* on the right, but that's a bit more complex. After you have the equation written, click the graph button in the lower-right corner of the screen. If you replace the equal sign with an inequality (< for less than, > for greater than, <= less than or equal and >= for greater than or equal), you'll get a shaded graph showing all of the pairs of *x* and *y* values that make the equation true.

If you include the pseudoconstant *n* on the right side of the equation, you get the animation control, which lets you display the graph while you vary the value for *n*. The animation effect comes into play because the shape and size of the graph changes as you change *n*. You can either change the value for *n* by dragging the slide bar or have your Mac change the value automatically by clicking the right-pointing triangle on the control. (Familiar to stereo-equipment users as the start button.) If you click the button labeled *n*, you can set the range of values used to vary *n*. (I called it a pseudoconstant because it's used like a constant in the equation, but constants aren't supposed to vary. That's the job of variables.)

To create a three-dimensional graph, start your equation with *Z*= and then use an equation that is written in terms of *x* and *y* or one that uses radius and theta.

More Stuff

TIP

You need to use lowercase letters for all of your variables or else you'll confuse your poor Mac and it will refuse to graph.

Apple menu⇨Jigsaw Puzzle

Gives you an opportunity to waste time while learning world geography. This is a particularly useful program for those of you who believe the world is flat — the picture proves it.

Just the facts

To get started, open the puzzle by choosing Apple menu⇨Jigsaw Puzzle and then choose Options⇨Start New Puzzle (or press ⌘-N). You are then faced with the toughest decision — what size pieces to use. Your choices are Small, Medium, or Large. Click the choice you want and then click OK. To move a piece, position the cursor over it, hold down the button, and move it to the new location. If you put it in the right place, when you release the mouse button, the puzzle piece snaps into position and blends in with any other pieces around it.

If you need help, you can choose Options⇨Show Picture. (Click in the close box to get rid of the sample picture.) If you just want to be entertained, or if the puzzle proves too much, you can choose Options⇨Solve Puzzle. When you're done, choose File⇨Quit.

More Stuff

TIP

If you get tired of working with the world map, you can actually create your own jigsaw puzzles by copying a picture onto the Clipboard (select the picture and then choose Edit⇨Copy), choosing Apple menu⇨Jigsaw Puzzle, and then pasting the picture onto the current puzzle (by choosing Edit⇨Paste). The shape of the puzzle automatically adjusts to the shape of the picture. There are several very nice images in the Scrapbook (accessed via the Apple menu).

NOTE

If you want, you can select a different background color for the border by using Options⇨Set Background Color (or by pressing ⌘-B). If you need to work quietly in your office, you might want to turn the sound off by choosing Options⇨Use Sound Effects (or by pressing ⌘-E). A check next to the option means that the sound is on; no check means that you can play silently.

Apple menu⇨Key Caps

Shows you the various characters available from the keyboard in any of the fonts installed on your system. Although you can cut and paste the information from the Key Caps window, this desk accessory is more useful as a way to decide what font to use in your word processing or desktop publishing program.

Just the facts

After you choose Apple menu⇨Key Caps, your screen shows a copy of your keyboard floating in a window. In addition, there is a Key Caps menu in the menu bar. Unless you have pressed Caps Lock, the keyboard on the screen displays the lowercase letters. (With Caps Lock pressed, it displays the uppercase letters.) You can either use the mouse pointer to click keys on the on-screen keyboard, or you can simply press the keys on your physical keyboard. As you press a key, the character that it currently represents is displayed across the top of the window.

The Key Caps menu lists all of the fonts that are currently available on your Macintosh. After selecting one, the characters on the screen's keyboard change to show you what that font looks like. Some of the fonts don't produce letters. These are called decorative fonts and are used to separate sections of a document, as bullets for a list or whatever your imagination can come up with. You could even use them as a secret code for writing to your friends.

To see the other available characters within a font, press any combination of the Shift and Option keys. There are four sets of characters that you can see: characters with no modifier key pressed, with Shift pressed, with Option pressed, and with both Shift and Option pressed together. By pressing the various key combinations, you can often find the character that you are searching for. Remember what keys you had to press and then close Key Caps. Back in your document, make sure you are using the same font as the one you used in Key Caps and then press the same set of keys to get the character you want.

More Stuff

TIP

Some characters have a thicker border around the key on the screen, which indicates that the character is intended for use in combination with a second character. You press the key for the character with the thicker border and then the key for the character you want to combine it with. One example is Option-E, which displays the accent mark. To combine the accent with the letter E, press Option-E and then the E. (Don't hold down the Shift key; use lowercase Es for both.)

Apple menu⇨Mail and Catalogs

Opens up the exciting world of network mail and workgroup computing. Roughly translated, you can now send memos and reports electronically that will sit in someone's In basket until it's too late and, even more useful, you now have an electronic In basket where you can let things sit. This command only appears if PowerTalk is installed on your Macintosh.

Just the facts

Using Apple menu⇨Mail and Catalogs is covered in Part 8.

Apple menu⇨Note Pad

Just perfect for jotting down those little notes to yourself, the notepad has eight separate pages that you can use. The other neat thing about the System 7.5 notepad is that it works with clipping files. For more information about clippings, see "Using desktop clippings" under "Desktop Things" in Part 1.

Just the facts

Choose Apple menu⇨Notepad and start typing to put things on the first page. If you want to move to another page, you'll need to turn the page by clicking the page corner in the lower-left of the notepad. You click the page that's in the background to move back a page. The following figure has the two page corners neatly labeled.

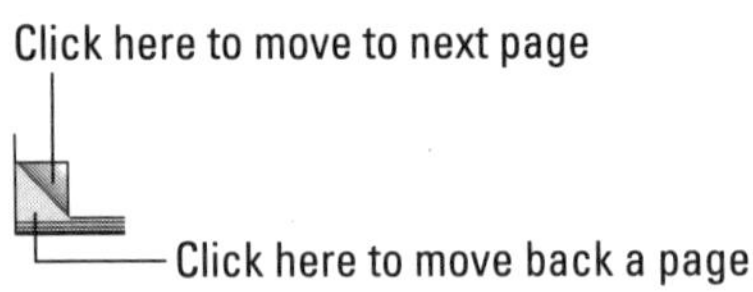

Each page can hold as much information as you want. Unlike a word processor, Notepad doesn't move information between pages to make them fit on the printed page. Instead, each page is like a separate document.

More Stuff

NEW 7.5 You can change the font used in the notepad by choosing Edit⇨Preferences and using the drop-down lists. Every page in the notepad uses the same font.

The notepad is now even more useful for keeping little notes to yourself because you can search the current page or all of the pages to a particular bit of text. To perform a search, choose Edit⇨Find (or press ⌘-F) and then enter the text you are looking for. Next, choose between looking Just in this note or In all the notes by clicking the appropriate option. Finally, click Find to begin looking. If the first match isn't the one you were looking for, you can choose Edit⇨Find Again (or press ⌘-G) to look again.

Apple menu⇨Recent Applications

NEW 7.5 Switches to any of your recently used programs without requiring you to track down the icon for that program. All you need to do is choose the program's name from the submenu and your Mac opens it right up.

Just the facts

The first step is to select the Apple menu and move your cursor so that the Recent Applications command is highlighted. If your Mac is set up to use submenus (with the Apple Menu Options control panel), a list of recent applications appears to the right of the Apple menu. Move your cursor onto the list and then up or down to select the program you want. When the program's name is highlighted, release the mouse button and the program starts.

If your Mac isn't using Apple menu submenus, you can choose the Recent Applications command to open a folder showing aliases for the programs you've used recently. If you hold down the Option key while double-clicking the icon for the program you want, the program opens and the window with the aliases closes behind you. If you want to leave the window open, double-click the icon without holding down the Option key.

More Stuff

NOTE Aliases for each of the recent applications are stored in the Recent Applications folder, which is inside of the Apple Menu Items folder, which is within the System Folder.

For information on turning on or off Apple menu submenus and setting the number of applications shown in the Recent Applications folder, see the entry for the Apple Menu Options control panel in Part 4.

Apple menu⇨Recent Documents

Opens a document you've used recently. If the program for the document isn't already opened, your Mac first opens the program and then the document.

Just the facts

Open the Apple menu and move your cursor so that the Recent Document command is highlighted. If a list of recent documents appears to the right of the Apple menu, it means that you're using submenus (turned on with the Apple Menu Options control panel) and you can just choose the document from the list. Move your cursor onto the list and then up or down to highlight the document you want to open. When the document's name is highlighted, release the mouse button; the document and, if necessary, its associated program open.

If you don't get a submenu when you highlight Recent Documents, just let up on the mouse button. That opens the folder showing aliases for all of the documents you've used recently. Hold down the Option key while double-clicking the icon for the document you want. This action opens the document and, if necessary, its parent program and also closes the window behind you. If you don't hold down the Option key, the document still opens, but the window doesn't close behind you.

More Stuff

Like the recent applications and recent servers, each of the recent documents has an alias stored in a folder within the Apple Menu Item folder. For documents, the folder's name is Recent Documents.

For information on turning on or off Apple menu submenus and setting the number of documents shown in the Recent Documents folder, see the entry for the Apple Menu Options control panel in Part 4.

Apple menu⇨Recent Servers

NEW 7.5

Reconnects your Mac to a recently used server. Any passwords that you normally provide are still required.

Just the facts

When you highlight Recent Servers on the Apple menu, one of two things happens. If you are using submenus, a menu with your recent servers appears to the right. Move your cursor over to the menu and then choose the server name that you want. If a submenu doesn't appear, then you need to choose Recent Servers to open a window with aliases for all of the servers you've used recently. Double-click the server you want and your Mac starts the connection process.

More Stuff

WARNING!

The only disadvantage to the Recent Servers feature is that someone else using your Mac can use the aliases of the recent servers to reconnect to the servers you use, especially if you store your password with the connection. If you are responsible for maintaining the privacy of the servers you use, you probably shouldn't use the Recent Servers feature. You can use the Apple Menu Options control panel to turn the feature on or off.

NOTE

Aliases for the recent servers are stored in the Recent Servers folder within the Apple Menu Items folder.

REFERENCE

For information on turning on or off Apple menu submenus and setting the number of servers shown in the Recent Servers folder, see the entry for the Apple Menu Options control panel in Part 4.

Apple menu⇨Scrapbook

Gives you a place to store odds and ends that you might want to use in your various programs. The Scrapbook can hold text, pictures, sounds, and a few other types of information. Because it's on the Apple menu, you can open the Scrapbook easily from within other programs.

Just the facts

Choosing Apple menu⇨Scrapbook opens your current Scrapbook file. If you want to use an item from the Scrapbook, first find the item by using the scroll bar along the bottom. The information at the bottom of the window tells you how many items are in the

Scrapbook as well as the type and size of the current item. For some items, there's additional information. For example, with sounds you see how long the sound is (duration).

The old-fashioned method for using the Scrapbook still works. You can cut or copy items in documents and paste them in the Scrapbook, and you can cut or copy items in the Scrapbook and paste them in documents. For more on moving information using this method, see Edit⇨Cut, Edit⇨Copy, and Edit⇨Paste.

NEW 7.5 Many newer Macintosh programs also support a drag-and-drop technique. Position the Scrapbook and document windows so that you can see both the item you want from the Scrapbook and the location where you want to put it. Put your cursor over the Scrapbook item, hold down the mouse button, and move the cursor to where you want the item. When you release the mouse button, the item is copied from the Scrapbook into the document. The object is always pasted full-size, so you can change the size of the Scrapbook window if necessary.

Note that you can also drag and drop items from other programs into the Scrapbook if that program supports System 7.5's drag-and-drop feature. The Notepad is one such program. You can drag and drop text from the Notepad to the Scrapbook and vice versa. Give it a try.

More Stuff

NOTE The items in the Scrapbook are actually kept in the Scrapbook file, which can be found in the System Folder. The actual Scrapbook program is kept in the Apple Menu Items folder.

REFERENCE System 7.5 offers another technique for storing stray bits of information. For more information, see "Using desktop clippings" under "Desktop Things" in Part 1.

Apple menu⇨•Shut Down

NEW 7.5 Performs the exact same command as Special⇨Shut Down. It prepares your Mac to be turned off and, on many models, actually turns off the Mac. Because this command is now on the Apple menu as well as the Special menu, it's available even when you're not working in the Finder.

Just the facts

When you choose Apple menu⇨•Shut Down, your Mac checks for any changes that you haven't saved, asks about saving those changes (if any), and then closes all of your programs. Next, it makes sure that all of your files are safely stored on disk and either turns off the power (on some models) or tells you that it's OK to turn off the power (on other models).

More Stuff

There are a few more details discussed under the entry for Special⇨Shut Down.

Apple menu⇨Stickies

Puts notes of various colors all over your screen. Fortunately, these notes are the electronic kinds so you don't have to worry about getting the glue off of your monitor.

Just the facts

To turn Stickies on temporarily, choose Apple menu⇨Stickies. You may see a number of small, pastel-colored windows on your screens with messages. The first time you use Stickies on your Mac, you'll see several notes from Apple about how to use them.

There are two things you must understand about how Stickies work to avoid becoming confused about storing your notes. The first is that anything you write on a stickie is automatically saved when you quit the program — you don't have to do anything. That's great; you don't worry about remembering File⇨Save or any other command. The other thing that you need to know is that anytime you close a stickie, the information is thrown away, so you need to be extra careful to avoid losing things. Now, that's if you close an individual note. If you turn off the feature entirely (by choosing File⇨Quit), any notes that are still on your screen are automatically saved.

In most programs, when you close a file, you get a reminder about saving changes. Not so with Stickies. Whether you get a message at all is controlled by the Confirm window-closing option under Edit⇨Preferences. With a check next to Confirm window-closing, whenever you close a window, you get a dialog box with three choices. The first is Don't Save, which just closes the stickie and throws away the information. The next is Cancel, which keeps the stickie on your desktop (and cancels the request you made to close the note). The third is Save, which is a bit misleading. Rather than saving the information as a stickie, the Save option opens a dialog box which you use to create a text file with the text from the stickie.

When you have a stickie selected, the four Stickies menus appear in the menu bar. The File menu contains the same sort of commands you'd expect in any program. Although all changes are automatically saved when you quit Stickies, you can use File⇨Save All to save any changes you've made that you want to be sure not to lose. (See the next paragraph for info on how to automatically save your notes when you move to another program from Stickies.) Choosing File⇨Export Text is the same as closing a stickie and then clicking the Save button. Both create a text file with the stickie's contents. File⇨Import Text can be used to take the information from a text file and put it onto a stickie.

The Edit command is very standard with a couple of additional commands at the bottom. Edit⇨Use As Default takes the formatting of the current stickie and uses it for any new stickies you create. This feature is useful if you have format you particularly like. Edit⇨Preferences is used to control some aspects of how the program behaves. Options under this command include Confirm window-closing (which I covered earlier in this entry) and Launch at system startup (which is covered in the first tip in "More Stuff"). A check next to the Save All on deactivate option causes all of your notes to be saved when you move to another program. This feature makes it more likely that your notes will have been saved in the event of a system crash. The Zoom-box collapses window option controls whether the window shrinks to just its title bar when you collapse a note. When this box is cleared, clicking a note's zoom box shrinks the window to a much smaller size, as you would normally expect. When this option is checked, clicking a note's zoom box collapses the window so that only the title bar is visible, much like when you use the new WindowShade feature on a typical window. Holding down the Option key when clicking a note's zoom box temporarily toggles between the two window-collapsing options.

Note⇨Text Style opens a dialog box for setting the various attributes for the text within a note. You can specify the text's font, size, and style. Note⇨Note Info tells you when the note was created and when it was last modified.

The Color menu is used for selecting the color for the stickie's background.

More Stuff

TIP

If you decide that you really like using Stickies and want to keep them on all the time, choose Edit⇨Preferences and put a check next to the Launch at system startup option. With this option activated, every time you start up your computer, Stickies launches automatically. Apple really believes that you should like the Stickies feature. The first time you turn off Stickies (by choosing File⇨Quit), you are asked if you want the notes to reappear when you start up your Mac. Clicking Yes is the same as setting the option just described.

For a description of using Stickies on your desktop, see "Putting a stickie on your desktop" under "Desktop Things" in Part 1.

Application menu⇨Application List

Switches from the current program to another program. Only programs that are currently running appear on the *application list*. The reason that application list is in italic is that there isn't really a command of that name. Instead, the bottom portion of the Application menu lists all of the programs that are currently running. Of course, there's no menu named *Application* either. It's the menu on the far right.

Just the facts

To switch to another program that's already running, open the Applications menu (the menu on the far right) and then choose the program you want from the list at the bottom of the menu. If the program you want isn't listed, it isn't currently running, which means that you need to go to the Finder to launch the program (or maybe you can launch the program from a hierarchical submenu on the Apple menu if you have it so configured).

More Stuff

The application menu is always located on the far right of the title bar and is represented by an icon. Its icon changes to match the current program. If it looks like a little Macintosh, that means you're working on the desktop in the Finder. If you don't recognize the icon, check the bottom of the Application menu — the current program has a check next to its name.

To hide the current program as you move to another program, hold down the Option key as you choose the other program's name.

Application menu⇨Hide Finder

Hides the current program's windows. You might be wondering about the italic for the word Finder in the heading. Well, the name of the command changes to reflect which program is current. That way, if you're currently in the Finder, the command is Hide Finder, but if you're working with the Scrapbook, the command is Hide Scrapbook.

Just the facts

Pull down the Application menu (the one on the far right of the menu bar) and choose the first command to hide the current program's window. The name of the command reflects what program will be hidden. For example, if you're working on the desktop, the command is Hide Finder. If you are working with the Notepad, the command is Hide Notepad.

More Stuff

NOTE

Each program has its own layer on the desktop with the one current program always being on top of the stack. When you hide the current program, the one under it becomes active.

I guess you could call the Application menu the Chameleon menu. The icon it uses to represent itself changes to match the current program. Because the name of the Hide command also changes to match the program, maybe it should be called the Chameleon command on the Chameleon menu. Good luck in tracking it down.

NOTE

When a program is hidden, its icon appears in a lighter gray on the Application menu.

Application menu⇨Hide Others

Makes any windows for programs other than the current one disappear. This command is very useful if you are distracted by the contents of the other windows and need to focus on your work (for example, when you need to hide that game you were just playing).

Just the facts

To hide everything except windows for the current program, choose Hide Others from the Application menu (the one represented by an icon and located at the far right of the menu bar). All of the other windows for other applications disappear. Other windows for the current program remain visible.

More Stuff

NOTE

The Application menu can be a bit hard to recognize. It's always represented by an icon and it's always located on the far right of the title bar. What makes it hard to recognize is that the icon changes to match the current program. If it looks like a little Macintosh, that means you're working on the desktop in the Finder. Otherwise, if you don't recognize the icon, check the bottom of the Application menu. The program with a check next to its name is the current program.

TIP It's often easier to simply zoom the current window so that it takes up all of the screen. To do that, click once in the zoom box (located in the upper-right corner of the window). If the window still doesn't take up the full screen, use the size box in the lower-right corner to extend the window even further. For more information, see "Window Things" in Part 1.

TIP If you select a program from the application list, it is no longer hidden. If you want to move to another program and hide the first, the easiest way is to hold down the Option key while choosing the other program from the application list. Holding down the Option key hides the current program as soon as you leave it.

NOTE The various icons on the desktop are not within any window. You can control whether they are visible when you are not working with the Finder by using the General Controls control panel.

REFERENCE To get the other windows back, you can either choose the program you want from the Application menu (see Application menu⇨*Application List*) or choose the Show All command (also on the Application menu).

Application Menu⇨Show All

Displays the windows from any hidden programs. This command makes your screen a bit more cluttered but lets you see everything that you are working with.

Just the facts

Choose Show All from the Application menu (the icon at the far right of the menu bar) and the windows for each of the programs that are currently running show themselves. Of course, some windows may still be covered up by those from other programs, so you may have to move windows around to find the one you want.

More Stuff

NOTE The icons for hidden programs appear in a lighter gray on the Application menu.

REFERENCE To find out how things get hidden, see Application Menu⇨Hide Others or Application Menu⇨Hide *Finder*. For information about moving between programs, see Application Menu⇨*Application List*. To find out about hiding or showing items that are on the desktop while you are working with a program, see the General Controls control panel in Part 4.

Edit⇨Clear

Completely and utterly destroys whatever is selected. While Edit⇨Cut gently removes the selected information and puts it onto the Clipboard, Edit⇨Clear just rips it out, roots and all, and tosses it onto the great electronic compost pile. It's gone. You can't get it back. OK, if you immediately select Edit⇨Undo, it might come back, but you need to do it immediately.

Just the facts

Highlight what you want to get rid of and then choose Edit⇨Clear. It's so easy to use, it's almost dangerous.

More Stuff

TIP: In many programs, you can use ⌘-B as a shortcut for Edit⇨Clear, but this shortcut doesn't work within the Finder.

REFERENCE: If you want to move information, you can use Edit⇨Cut and Edit⇨Paste or the new technique described in "Using desktop clippings" under "Desktop Things" in Part 1.

Edit⇨Copy

Puts a copy of the selected information on the Clipboard, leaving the original intact. You can then use Edit⇨Paste to put the information somewhere else in your document (or into another document). Although this command is probably most useful within programs, you can use it within the Finder as well.

For keyboard krazies

⌘ + C

or

F3

Just the facts

Highlight whatever it is you want to make a copy of, choose Edit⇨Copy (or press one of the keyboard shortcuts), and you've got an exact duplicate stored on the Clipboard. Now, move to where you want to put the copy and choose Edit⇨Paste. It's OK if you perform other tasks or use other commands before pasting as long as you *don't* put something else onto the Clipboard.

The wonder of the Macintosh and its Clipboard is that the Clipboard can hold almost anything. Not only can you copy information within your document, but between documents — even those created in different programs. All you need to know is how to use the few commands on the Edit menu. Your Macintosh takes care of making sure that information is formatted so that it can be used in multiple documents.

More Stuff

WARNING! The most common mistake people (including me) make when using the Edit menu is forgetting that the Clipboard can only hold one thing. If you put something on the Clipboard, be sure to paste it somewhere else in your document (using Edit⇨Paste) before you try to put something else on the Clipboard (with either Edit⇨Cut or Edit⇨Copy). Actually, accidentally putting something new on the Clipboard isn't a big problem when you are copying information because you can always go back and make another copy of the original information.

NOTE If you select an icon on the desktop or in a window, only the name of the icon will be copied when you choose Edit⇨Copy. To actually make a copy of an icon (and the file or folder it represents), you need to use one of the techniques described in "File Things" in Part 1. These same techniques work with folders, as described in "Folder Things." To copy just part of an icon's name, click the name, wait for the background to change, and then select the desired part of the name.

REFERENCE If you need a temporary place to hold something, you can look at either Apple menu⇨Scrapbook or Apple menu⇨Notepad. In System 7.5, there's another way to copy information; it involves things called *desktop clippings*. I cover them in "Using desktop clippings" under "Desktop Things" in Part 1. To remove something from a document and put it on the Clipboard, use Edit⇨Cut. To place something from the Clipboard into a document, use Edit⇨Paste.

Edit⇨Cut

Takes whatever is selected, removes it and places it on the Clipboard. You usually use this command within programs, but it works the same way on the desktop. If you have an icon on the desktop selected, it's the name that is taken and put on the Clipboard. Most other times, it's the entire item, whether it's text, a picture, or sound. You use Edit⇨Paste to get the information off of the Clipboard and into your document.

For keyboard krazies

⌘ + X

or

F2

Just the facts

Highlight what it is you want to put on the Clipboard, choose Edit⇨Cut (or press one of the keyboard shortcuts) and what you have highlighted disappears from your screen. Don't worry though — it's just been stored on the Clipboard, so it's still available. You can now use Edit⇨Paste to insert the contents of the Clipboard somewhere else.

The most important thing to understand about using Edit⇨Cut and the Clipboard to move information is that you are not restricted to moving the item within the current document. You can move it to almost any other document, even a document in another program. For example, you might use the Clipboard to move a picture into your word processing document and then use that exact same Clipboard to copy in part of a spreadsheet. Your Macintosh takes care of all of the secret electronic paperwork involved in moving information with different formats.

More Stuff

NOTE

The Clipboard can only hold one thing at a time, so be careful. If you use Edit⇨Cut to place something onto the Clipboard, you need to use Edit⇨Paste to put the contents somewhere before you use either Edit⇨Copy or Edit⇨Cut a second time. You don't have to paste the contents right away, but you do have paste it before it gets replaced by something else. Both Edit⇨Cut and Edit⇨Copy use the same Clipboard.

TIP — If you just need some place to store the contents of the Clipboard while you do something else, you can use either Apple menu⇨Scrapbook or Apple menu⇨Notepad. Both of these programs are available on the Apple menu and hold many types of information.

NEW 7.5 — System 7.5 offers a new way of moving information between programs. It uses what are called clipping files. I cover this new technology under "Using desktop clippings" in the "Desktop Things" section of Part 1.

WARNING! — A very few programs, notably some versions of Microsoft Excel, don't immediately remove the information you cut. Instead, the program marks the information with a dashed rectangle and only moves it to the new location when you choose Edit⇨Paste. There are some technical reasons that this program has to work in this way, but it's still a little bit confusing and quite strange.

TIP — If you are working with icons, clicking an icon actually just selects its name for cutting or copying. If you choose Edit⇨Cut, the name disappears, but the icon (as well as the file or folder it represents) remains unchanged. To make a copy of a file or folder, you should use Edit⇨Duplicate or one of the methods covered in "File Things" in Part 1. If you want to delete an icon (and the file or folder it represents), drag it to the Trash. If you select part of an icon's name and cut it, only the part you selected is removed and put on the Clipboard.

REFERENCE — If you want to leave the original information where you found it, use Edit⇨Copy, which duplicates the information and puts the copy on the Clipboard. To move information off of the Clipboard and into your document, you use Edit⇨Paste. To get rid of selected information entirely, without changing what's already on the Clipboard, use Edit⇨Clear.

Edit⇨Paste

Takes whatever is on the Clipboard and inserts it where you are currently working. You need to have put something on the Clipboard by using Edit⇨Cut or Edit⇨Copy. If you highlight something before choosing Edit⇨Paste, whatever you selected is replaced when you paste in the Clipboard's contents.

For keyboard krazies

⌘ + V

or

F4

Just the facts

If you want to insert the information from the Clipboard, click once where you want the new stuff to go and then choose Edit⇨Paste. If you want to replace something with what's on the Clipboard, highlight what's to be replaced and then choose Edit⇨Paste. In either case, you can use the keyboard shortcuts (⌘-V or F4) instead of the menu command if you so desire.

More Stuff

There's a new and improved method for copying information. I cover this feature in "Using desktop clippings" under "Desktop Things" in Part 1.

To get something on the Clipboard, you need to use either Edit⇨Cut (which removes the original) or Edit⇨Copy (which leaves the original and uses a copy).

Edit⇨Select All

Selects everything it can get its grubby little paws on. This can mean every icon within a window or every item on the desktop. Now all you need to do is decide what you want to do with them.

For keyboard krazies

⌘ + A

Just the facts

It's pretty simple. Make sure that you're in the window that contains everything you want and then choose Edit⇨Select All (or press ⌘-A). Everything in the window, even those items not currently visible, is selected. What you do with them now is your business.

More Stuff

TIP

This command is probably most useful for making a copy of the contents of a disk or folder without copying the entire thing. If you just copy a floppy disk onto your hard disk, the information appears in its own folder. If you open the disk window, select everything, and then copy those items, you can put them within a folder that already exists on your system.

Edit⇨Show Clipboard

Reveals whatever is currently on the Clipboard. Trust me, this command becomes much more useful as you start to get older and can no longer juggle thirty different tasks in your head at one time.

Just the facts

When you choose Edit⇨Show Clipboard, a window opens showing you what's on the Clipboard. If you look in the upper-left corner of the Clipboard window just below the title bar, you'll find a note that tells you what type of information is currently on the Clipboard.

More Stuff

NOTE

You can leave the Clipboard open and watch the contents change as you use the Edit⇨Cut and Edit⇨Copy commands.

Edit⇨Undo

Takes back your last editing action. This command is your Mac's reverse gear. You can take one step backward and pretend that whatever change you just made never happened.

For keyboard krazies

⌘ + Z

or

F1

Just the facts

If you make a mistake, immediately choose Edit⇨Undo (or press one of the keyboard shortcuts). Do not pass Go. Do not wait for further instructions. Just do it!

More Stuff

If choosing Edit⇨Undo seems to cause more problems than it cures, try choosing it again. In most situations, that undoes the Undo, which means that you're back where you started before first choosing Edit⇨Undo.

Some programs now offer what is called a multilevel undo. This feature enables you to back out of several actions. System 7.5 doesn't offer multiple undos on the desktop, but it doesn't prevent programs from having this feature. Be careful, because in programs that allow multiple undos, there is a separate command for reversing an undo (usually called something like Edit⇨Redo).

The key word in this description is an *editing* action, which means a change you make to text or the contents of a document. Most of the actions you do on the desktop, such as deleting a file or moving a folder to a new location, *cannot* be reversed with Edit⇨Undo.

File⇨Close Window

Closes the current window so that you can move to another. You need to close windows occasionally or else your desktop will become so crowded you won't find anything.

For mouse maniacs

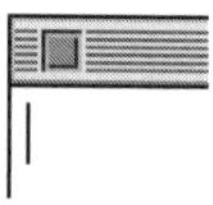

For keyboard krazies

⌘ + W

Just the facts

You can choose File⇨Close Window, press ⌘-W, or click in the close box in the left corner of the title bar. It doesn't matter which you do; the window closes.

More Stuff

If you just want to get the window out of the way for a moment, System 7.5 offers a neat way of temporarily closing up most of the window. You roll up the window shade. Just double-click the window's title bar (at the very top of the window where its name is). For more information on this trick, see "Rolling up the window shade" under "Window Things" in Part 1. By the way, to unroll the window shade and get your window back, double-click the title bar again.

File⇨Duplicate

Makes a copy of the file in the same window. You generally want to use this command when you are going to rename the copy and make changes, leaving your original file intact.

For keyboard krazies

⌘ + D

Just the facts

You need to select the file you want to copy and then choose File⇨Duplicate (or press ⌘-D). The copy is created with the word *copy* at the end of the name. If the word *copy* is already there, the name will end with *copy 2*. After that, you get *copy 3*, *copy 4* and so on.

If you want to rename the file, click the name and wait for the color behind the name to change from black to your highlight color. To delete part of the name, highlight what you want to get rid of and press Delete. To insert something, click where you want to add the text and start typing. When you're done, you can just click something else or press Return.

More Stuff

When you make a copy of a locked file, the copy is not locked. Your Mac behaves in this way so that you can easily make a copy of a locked file to which you can make changes. Just remember that the copy is not protected from being deleted. For more information on locking files, see File⇨Get Info.

If you want to make a copy of the file on another disk, just drag the file to the other disk. If you want to copy something to another folder, hold down the Option key and then drag the file to the other folder. Both of these techniques are discussed under "File Things" in Part 1. If you want a copy of the file to keep just its icon in another place, you should probably use File⇨Make Alias.

File⇨Find

NEW 7.5

Finds that file you were working on just the other day and which you know is around here somewhere, but you just can't put your hands on it. Now, if they'd just develop a similar tool for use with my paper files.

For keyboard krazies

⌘ + F

Just the facts

The new, improved File⇨Find command gives you even more choices for describing the file you're looking for. At first glance, the Find File dialog box doesn't look all that impressive, but the key to its treasure chest of features is More Choices button in the lower-left corner. If you want to search for a file using more than one characteristic, click the More Choices button to add a new line for describing what you are looking for. You can have up to ten lines of characteristics. If you want to get rid of a line, click the Fewer Choices button (which isn't available if you only have one choice showing). You can also use the File⇨More Choices or File⇨Fewer Choices commands instead of the buttons.

To describe the file you want to find, you select a characteristic from the first column and a comparison from the second column. You then provide some type of information about what you're looking for. The information you provide can be a value you enter, a choice from a list, or a date you select using the standard Macintosh date formats. This handy-dandy table lists the characteristics you can use and the options available for each.

Characteristic	*Comparisons available*	*Compared to*
Name	contains (means the text can appear anywhere in the name) starts with (means text must appear as first characters — including spaces) ends with (means text must appear at last characters — including spaces) is (means text must match exactly — no extra characters) is not (means text must differ on at least one character) doesn't contain (means text must not appear in the name)	the text you type in
Kind	is is not	choice of alias, application, clipping file, document, folder, font, letter, sound, stationery
Label	is is not	any of the choices from the Label menu
Date Created or Date Modified	is is before is after is not is within a range of 1, 2, or 3 days, weeks or months or within 6 months	date you select
Size	is less than is greater than	a value in kilobytes
Version	is is not	a value you enter
Comments	contain do not contain	text you want to look for

(continued)

Characteristic	Comparisons available	Compared to
Lock Attribute	is	choice of: locked or unlocked
Folder Attribute	is is not	choice of: empty, shared or mounted
File Type	is is not	file type code (see the first tip in "More Stuff")
Creator	is	creator code (see the first tip in "More Stuff")

The more information you can provide about the file you're looking for, the fewer files you'll have to check before finding the one you want. Most of the characteristics are fairly obvious, but a few deserve special comment. The first choices in the list (Name, Kind, Label, Date Created and Date Modified) are generally the most useful. They're also the easiest to use. There are two things that need to be mentioned. First, the Date Modified is the lasttime you saved changes to the file, not the last time you looked at the file. Second, the letter option for the Kind characteristic locates any AppleMail documents on your Macintosh.

While Size, Version, and Comments are fairly straightforward to use, they're not as useful as many of the other choices. The problem is that you're unlikely to know the version or size of the file you're looking for. Furthermore, few people actually put information in the Comments box in an info window.

The Lock Attribute refers to whether the Locked check box is checked in the Get Info window for the file. I have no idea why the phrasing in the Find File dialog box is so awkward, but it's really a fairly simply concept. The choices for Folder Attribute are empty (there's nothing at all in the folder), shared (someone else is using the folder over the network), and mounted (you're using a folder on someone else's machine). The fact that you only use one of the choices makes the use of this characteristic somewhat limited, particularly because you may want to look for a shared folder that is also empty.

The File Type and Creator choices require that you know secret nerd information about the file codes. A method for finding out some of this information is covered in the first tip in "More Stuff."

After you click the Find button, all of the files that match the characteristics you select are displayed in an Items Found window like the one shown here.

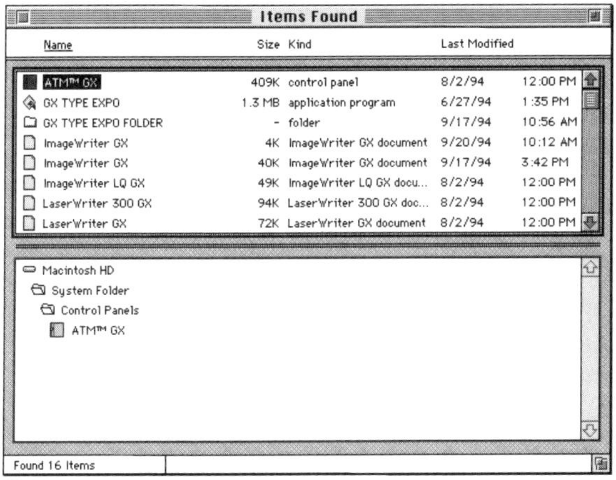

The Items Found window is much more than just a list of files. You can select one of the items (either a file or folder) listed in the top, and the bottom portion shows you the location of that item. You can double-click one of the files in the top portion of the window to open the file. If you double-click a folder or file in the bottom portion, a window for the folder opens. (If you double-click a file, the folder containing that file opens.) Use the View menu to change the order of the items listed in the top portion of the window.

You can also select a file (by clicking it once) and choose a command from the File menu. Your choices include File⇨Get Info, File⇨Print Item, and File⇨Open Item. File⇨Print Item works the same way as File⇨Print, and File⇨Open Item is the same as File⇨Open.

If you select a group of items (either by dragging across the group you want to select or by clicking the first item and then holding down the Shift key as you click items to add them to the group), you can open or print the entire group (although the File menu commands still say Print Item and Open Item rather than *Items*).

The Items Found window works like any other Macintosh window with one exception. You can change the position of the line dividing the top and bottom portions. To do that, place the cursor over the line and wait for it to turn into a small hand. When the hand appears, hold down the mouse button and move the mouse to move the desired position for the line. Release the mouse button when the line is where you want it.

The Find File dialog box remains open while you work with the Items Found dialog box. You can close either of them independently either by clicking in the window's close box or by choosing File⇨Close. You can close both of dialog boxes by choosing File⇨Quit. As soon as you close both windows, the Find File menus also disappear. To change which window you are working with, you can either click the window you want to use or choose File⇨Find to move from the Items Found window to the Find File dialog box.

More Stuff

TIP The most nerdy type of searches are for the File Type or Creator Type. These are special codes that are assigned to each and every file created on your Macintosh. The File Type code describes, not too surprisingly, what type of file it is. The Creator Type is a code used by the system to identify the program that created the file. One way to see the available file types is to open the PC Exchange control panel and click the Add button. Use the dialog box to select an application, and the list on the far right (labeled Document Type) shows all of the file types that can be created by that program. Each of the file types is shown with the document icon used for that type of file. Be sure to click the Cancel button to avoid adding an unnecessary PC Exchange definition.

NOTE If you really hate change, or if you just preferred the way System 7 originally searched for and found files, you can hold down the Shift key while selecting File⇨Find to get the old Find dialog box (or you can hold down the Shift key and press ⌘-F). If you want to remove the new File⇨Find feature entirely, remove the Find File extension from your Extensions folder within your System Folder.

TIP You can also search for a file using the same Find File utility by choosing Apple menu⇨Find File. This command is on the Apple menu as well as the File menu so that you can get to it from other programs.

NOTE You can change the font used for the Find File and Items Found dialog boxes by choosing Edit⇨Preferences when either dialog box is open.

REFERENCE To find out a bit more about the process of searching for a file, see "Finding a lost file" under "File Things" in Part 1. The File⇨Get Info and File⇨Sharing commands, which are available while working with Find File, are the same as those available normally and are discussed under their own entries. (Actually, even though it has a command reference entry, File⇨Sharing is discussed more fully in Part 8.)

File⇨Find Again

The File⇨Find Again command is only useful if you are using the old version of File⇨Find. There are two ways that you can access the old Find File:

- You don't have the Find File Extension in your Extension folder (in other words, the new File⇨Find isn't installed).
- You hold down the Shift key while choosing the File⇨Find or File⇨Find Again command.

For keyboard krazies

If the Find File Extension isn't installed:

⌘ + G

If the Find File Extension is installed:

⌘ + Shift + G

Just the facts

The fact is that this command is a bit confusing. Sorry. This File⇨Find Again command is designed to work with the old, pre-System 7.5 version of File⇨Find. With that version, you moved from one matching file to another each time you chose File⇨Find Again. With the System 7.5 version of File⇨Find, you get a list of all of the matches at once, so you don't need File⇨Find Again. It's only useful if you decide to use the old version of File⇨Find.

If you want to go back to always using the older version of Find File, simply open your System Folder (it's the one with a little Macintosh on it) and then open your Extensions folder (it's the one with a little puzzle piece on it). Now, look for the File Find Extension; it's shaped like a puzzle piece with an image of a hard disk and a magnifying glass. Drag the file out of the Extensions folder. You might want to create a new folder to hold it named something like Unused Bits and Pieces, or you may want to trash it.

To temporarily use the older version of Find, hold down the Shift key while choosing File⇨Find (or press ⌘-Shift-F). Enter the search information and press Return. (I assume you know how since you're the one who decided to use the older version.) To find the next match, either hold down the Shift key and choose File⇨Find Again or press ⌘-Shift-G.

More Stuff

NOTE

If you have the File Find Extension installed and are therefore using the new System 7.5 version of File⇨Find, choosing File⇨Find Again without holding down any special keys is exactly the same as choosing File⇨Find.

REFERENCE

To find out about the new version of File⇨Find, look at the entry right before this one.

File⇨Get Info

Provides all that you generally need to know about a file on your Mac. Exactly what information is shown varies depending upon the type of file you selected before choosing this command. Exactly what type of information you get for documents and programs is detailed in the "Just the facts" section.

For keyboard krazies

⌘ + I

Just the facts

To see the information about a file, click the file to select it and then choose File⇨Get Info (or press ⌘-I). To close the resulting Info window, just click in the close box in the upper-left corner.

With all types of files, the Info window tells you what kind of file it is, the size of the file, where it's stored, the date it was created, when it was last modified, and any comments that have been stored with the file. There's also an option to lock the file to protect it. The contents of a locked file cannot be changed, and deleting a locked file requires an extra step. A check next to Locked is all that is needed to lock a file. To clear the Locked check box and unlock a file, click the check box again. To add or change a comment, simply edit the text in the Comments box.

With aliases, the Info window tells you the location of the original file (in addition to the location of the alias). This window also provides the Find Original button, which opens the window for the folder containing the original file. The original file is highlighted for you.

With documents, the Info window provides a check box that enables you to make the document into a Stationery pad, which you use as a template for other documents. When you try to open a document that is marked as a Stationery pad (with a check next to the option on the Get Info dialog box), you get a new, untitled document that contains any text and formatting contained in the Stationery pad.

With programs, The Info window provides a section for setting the program's memory requirements. If you're working with a printer icon, you can actually change the location information.

More Stuff

You can actually change the icon used for a file, folder, program, or disk with the Get Info window. The hardest part is creating the new icon. You can use a painting program, an image from the Scrapbook, or a copy of another icon. If you use a paint program, select the area you want to use as the icon and copy it to the Clipboard (using Edit⇨Copy). To use an image from the Scrapbook, open the Scrapbook (Apple menu⇨Scrapbook) and then choose Edit⇨Copy. If you want to use an icon from another file, open that file's Get Info dialog box, click the icon shown in the upper-left corner, and then choose Edit⇨Copy. With any of these methods, you place a copy of the icon you want to use on the Clipboard.

Now, open the Get Info window for the file you want to change and click the icon in the upper-left corner. Choose Edit⇨Paste and the information from the Clipboard is inserted as the icon. If what was on the Clipboard wasn't the same size as normal icon, it's adjusted to fit. When you close the Get Info window, your Macintosh uses the icon you added. To restore the original icon for a file, open the Get Info window, select the icon by clicking it once, and then choose Edit⇨Clear.

When you rebuild your desktop file, (and if you're a good Mac user, you do it every month or so), you'll lose all of your comments in all Info windows.

When you use File⇨Get Info for a desktop printer icon, you can change the location that is reported for the printer. This location is used in dialog boxes that describe the printer and isn't related to where the printing files are stored on your disk. You might enter something like *on the desk right next to my computer* for the location.

For more information about setting the memory requirements for applications, see Chapter 10 of *Macintosh System 7.5 For Dummies*.

To find out more about what you can do with File⇨Get Info when printing, see Part 7. To find out about File⇨Get Info and what it can do with a PowerTalk network, see Part 8.

File⇨Make Alias

Creates a second icon for a file so that you can have icons for the same file in several different locations. The file size for an alias is generally only a few K, so you won't waste disk space if you create several aliases for files or folders that you access often. Aliases are a useful way around the rule that you can't be in two places at once.

For keyboard krazies

⌘ + M

Just the facts

Click the original file and then choose File⇨Make Alias (or press ⌘-M). You now have a second file sitting on top of the first. Notice that the name of the second file is in italic and has the same name but with the word *alias* appended to the end. Alias files always have their names in italic to remind you of what they are. Your Macintosh has to add the word *alias* because no two files in the same folder can have the same name. If you move the file to another folder, you can get rid of the *alias* part of the name.

More Stuff

TIP: The most common places to put aliases are on the desktop and in the Apple Menu Items folder (which causes the alias to appear on the Apple menu). Of course, you can put an alias wherever you want.

WARNING!: Just remember that both an alias and its original icon open the same file. To make a copy of a file, you need to use either File⇨Duplicate or one of the techniques listed under "File Things" in Part 1.

NOTE: Throwing away the alias does not change anything about the original file. On the other hand, if you throw away the original file, its alias becomes useless and ought to be trashed as well.

TIP: To jump to the folder containing the original for an alias, click the alias, choose File⇨Get Info, and click Find Original button.

File⇨New Folder

Creates a new folder for your organizing pleasure. The folder is created in the current window (which generally means inside whichever folder you are working with). If you are working on the desktop, the new folder appears on the desktop, but is actually stored on one of your disks.

For keyboard krazies

⌘ + N

Just the facts

Choose File⇨New Folder (or press ⌘-N) and immediately start typing the new name for the folder. When the folder first appears, its name is untitled folder, which is pretty silly, so you want to change it right away.

REFERENCE

For another perspective (and a different set of instructions) for creating a new folder, see "Creating a new folder" in "Folder Things" in Part 1.

More Stuff

TIP

The ⌘-N shortcut also works in most Save and Save As dialog boxes. So even when there isn't a special button for creating a folder, those of us in the know can still make a folder of our own by pressing the secret keys (⌘-N).

File⇨Open

Gets you into things (sometimes into folders, sometimes into files, sometimes into trouble, but always into something). If you open a folder or a disk, you can see what's inside the disk.
If you open a program file, you start working with that program. If you open a document file, you open whichever program created the document and can start working with the document.

For mouse maniacs

Double-click the icon.

For keyboard krazies

⌘ + O

or

⌘ + ↓

Just the facts

This is one command where it's almost always easier to use one of the shortcuts. Sure, you can double-click whatever it is you want to open. (Put your cursor over the icon and then double-click the mouse button.) If you'd rather use a keyboard shortcut, click the icon once to select it and then press one of the keyboard shortcuts (either ⌘-O or ⌘-down arrow). If you really want to use the menu command, click once to select the icon and then choose File⇨Open. The "File Things," "Folder Things," and "Disk Things" sections of Part 1 each discuss how to use the Open command.

More Stuff

TIP: You can open several items at once by selecting them as a group first and then opening any one of the items in the group. To select a group of items, click the first one and then hold down the Shift key as you click each of the others you want to add to the group. To remove an item from the group, hold down the Shift key and click it.

REFERENCE: The ⌘-down arrow is an unusual shortcut, but it does work. It's most useful when you've learned the other keyboard shortcuts described in Part 3.

TIP: If you want to open an item and then close the window you are working with, you can do it all in one step. Hold down the Option key while you open the item, and the window that contains the item closes as the item opens.

File⇨Page Setup

Controls how your page is formatted when you are using the File⇨Print Window or File⇨Print Desktop commands.

Just the facts

Page Setup is discussed along with the other printing commands in Part 7.

File⇨Print

Prints the selected item or items. The capability to print multiple items is what makes this command so worthwhile. You can highlight a group of documents and print all of them with a single command. This works even if they were created with different programs.

For keyboard krazies

⌘ + P

Just the facts

After selecting the file or files you want to work with, choose File⇨Print (or press ⌘-P). The program(s) for the document opens and presents you with the Print dialog box for that document. If the document is ready to print, simply click the Print button and you're off. Otherwise, you'll need to use some of the options discussed in Part 8.

More Stuff

If you try to print several documents created with different programs, your Mac may run out of RAM (working memory). You need to have enough working memory to open each of the programs in order to do a batch print.

You can only print documents that can be opened by the programs you have on your Mac. If you don't have the program that created a document, there isn't an easy way to print the document. Your best bet is to try to find one of the programs you do have that can open the document and print it from within that program. You may have to open each of your programs and try opening the document from within the programs to find one that works.

The details on printing are covered Part 8.

File⇨Print Desktop

Makes a copy of the information showing on your desktop appear on a piece of paper. (OK, it may take more than once piece.) Unlike File⇨Print Window, you can't use the View menu to change how things are displayed — your desktop is always in icon view, so your printout shows a bunch of icons.

Just the facts

There's not a lot to the File⇨Print Desktop command. You go to the File menu. You choose Print Desktop. You click the Print button in the resulting dialog box. You're done and will soon be the bearer of a fine desktop printout.

More Stuff

TIP: When printing the desktop, it generally works best if you first use File⇨Page Setup to change the paper's orientation to one of the Landscape choices. Using a landscape orientation makes the printing area wider than it is tall, which is more likely to match your screen.

REFERENCE: The choices you can get by clicking the More Choices or Options button in the Print dialog box are discussed in Part 7. If you are working with the items in a window, the last option on the file menu is File⇨Print Window.

File⇨Print Window

Takes whatever is in the current window and puts it on paper. What's showing in your window is controlled by the View menu. What prints is everything that the window contains, even if it isn't large enough on-screen to show its entire contents.

Just the facts

First, decide what it is you want to see on the list and use the View menu to organize the window's contents. Unfortunately, no matter what you do, you'll get a printout of everything that's in the window, not just those items that are currently showing. If you're working with a list view, you can control whether the contents of the folders within the window are expanded or collapsed.

When everything is just perfect (or at least marginally acceptable), choose File⇨Print Window. In the subsequent Print dialog box, click Print and you should get a list very shortly.

More Stuff

TIP: If you are using a list view and the columns are too wide to fit on a single page, choose File⇨Page Setup before printing and enter a scaling value. Printing at 90 percent will usually allow all of the columns to fit on the page.

REFERENCE: You can use one of the list views to show the contents of several folders at one time. For more information, see "List Things" in the Part 1. I discuss the various options of the Print dialog box in Part 7. To print a picture of the desktop, use the File⇨Print Desktop command. When no windows are active, the Print Desktop command appears at the bottom of the File menu.

File⇨Put Away

Returns an icon that's been placed on the desktop to the folder where it's really stored. When a removable disk is selected, File⇨Put Away ejects the disk. With a volume selected, your Mac unmounts that volume.

For keyboard krazies

⌘ + Y

Just the facts

When you place a file or folder on the desktop, its icon appears as though it were attached to the desktop background of your Mac. In reality, the file or folder "remembers" where it came from and is still stored on your disk. If you select the icon and then choose File⇨Put Away (or press ⌘-Y), the file or folder returns to its original home. This command is particularly useful when you are cleaning up your desktop and want to remove a file from the desktop and place it where it belongs.

You can also use this command to get a file or folder out of the Trash and return the file or folder to its old location on your hard disk. This feature can be a real timesaver if the file was originally buried in several layers of folders. To use File⇨Put Away in this way, open the Trash and click the file or folder you want to put back on your hard disk. Choose File⇨Put Away (or press ⌘-Y) and the item's back where it belongs.

Finally, if you select a disk icon or volume icon and then choose File⇨Put Away (or press ⌘-Y), the disk is ejected or unmounted and its icon is removed from the desktop. This action is the same as dragging the disk or volume to the Trash.

More Stuff

REFERENCE

To physically eject the disk but keep its icon on the desktop, use Special⇨Eject Disk.

File⇨Sharing

Changes the access privileges of a folder for use with file sharing. You use the options presented with this command to control who on a network has access to your folders and what they're allowed to do when they connect.

Just the facts

REFERENCE

This command is discussed in detail in Part 8.

Label

Changes the label assigned to a file, which also changes the color of the icon's background. The choices on the Label menu are most often used to create a colorful look for a window, but they can actually be used for organization. The View⇨by Label command lets you sort your files based upon the label categories.

Just the facts

Select the file or group of files you want to label and then choose the label you want from the Label menu. That's really all there is to it.

More Stuff

NOTE

In order to display the name of the label in list views, you may have to change the settings in the Views control panel.

Use the Labels control panel to change the colors used for each group and the text associated with each label.

Special⇨Clean Up

Organizes the icons within a window or on the desktop. The name of the command changes depending upon whether you are in a window (or on the desktop) and whether you hold down the Option or Shift keys.

Just the facts

If you are working with items on the desktop, the first command on the Special menu is Clean Up Desktop. Choose it and all of the icons on the desktop move so that they are positioned on an invisible grid. The position of the grid is controlled by the Views control panel.

If you are working with items within a window, the first command on the Special menu is Clean Up Window. Select it and all of the icons within the active window are arranged on the grid (set using the Views control panel). The command is not available unless you are working with an icon view (either View⇨by Icon or View⇨by Small Icon).

If you select a group of icons (see the first tip in More Stuff) — either on the desktop or in a window — and hold down the Shift key while pulling down the Special menu, the first command is Clean Up Selection. Only those items that are in the selected group are moved so that they are arranged on the grid.

There's one more trick up the sleeve of Special⇨Clean Up. (Do commands have sleeves? Do commands even wear clothes? Oh well, never mind. On with the explanation…) If you are working with items in a window, you can hold down the Option key while pulling down the Special menu to get a command that both sorts the items and arranges them on the grid.

What you'll end up sorting on is determined by what list view you last used with the window. If you've never used a list view, holding down the Option key and pulling down the Special menu reveals the Clean Up by Name command, which sorts the icons by name and arranges them on the grid.

To sort by one of the other categories, display a list view sorted on that category (you can select it from the View menu) and then return to the icon view (by choosing View⇨by Icon or View⇨by Small Icon). Now, when you hold down the Option key and pull down the Special menu, the first command is for sorting by whatever category you just used. For example, to organize icons by size, first choose View⇨by Size. Then return to an icon view (by using View⇨by Icon or View⇨by Small Icon), hold down the Option key, and pull down the Special menu. The first command is now Clean Up by Size. This trick works with any of the list view categories on the View menu. You determine what categories are available on the View menu by using the Views control panel.

More Stuff

TIP You can select a group with one of two techniques. The first technique is to click the first item you want in the group and then hold down the Shift key as you click each additional item you want to put into the group. The second technique is to draw a selection marquee around the group. Move the cursor so that it's above and to left of all of the items you want in the group. Then hold down the mouse button and drag to the lower-right. As you move the cursor, it draws a blinking rectangle. Any item that is either enclosed or touched by the rectangle is included in the group. To remove an item from a group, hold down the Shift key and click the item to be removed.

TIP Use the Views control panel to determine the font and size for icon names in the Finder. The font size of icon names affects how close together the icons are placed when you use the Special⇨Clean Up command.

REFERENCE The Views control panel is covered in Part 4. For more on cleaning up the desktop, see "Desktop Things" in Part 1.

Special⇨Eject Disk

Physically ejects the disk from your Macintosh but leaves the disk icon on the desktop. This command is useful when you need to work with more than one disk and only have one disk drive.

For keyboard krazies

⌘ + E

Just the facts

First, click the icon for the disk you want to eject. Then choose Special⇨Eject Disk (or press ⌘-E). The disk pops out but its icon remains on the desktop.

More Stuff

WARNING! If you use a disk ejected with this command in any other machine and then try to return it to your Mac, your Mac may not recognize the disk. If this situation occurs, rather than using the disk icon that is already on the desktop, your Macintosh adds a new disk icon when you reinsert the disk. It's OK. After you're done with what you are working on, just throw out the first disk icon. If your Mac asks you to insert the disk at this point, press ⌘-period. (You may have to do it more than once.) This key combination is essentially the same as clicking a Cancel button, and it tells your Mac to give up whatever it is trying to do, including its persistent request for a disk.

TIP There are two additional shortcuts for ejecting disks. Use ⌘-Shift-1 to eject the disk in your primary floppy disk drive. Use ⌘-Shift-2 to eject the disk in your second floppy drive. Neither of these shortcuts will eject a CD from a CD-ROM drive.

TIP If you need to unmount a hard disk (that is, remove its icon from your desktop), just drag it to the Trash. Although your Mac doesn't spit out the hard disk, it does remove its icon from the desktop and pretends that the hard disk no longer exists. You can't unmount the hard disk that you use to start up your Mac (the one in the upper-right corner of the desktop).

REFERENCE If you want to eject a disk physically and remove its disk icon (which is the most common way to eject a disk) you can either drag the disk icon to the Trash or click the disk icon and choose File⇨Put Away.

Special⇨Empty Trash

Actually deletes the files that are currently stored in the Trash. Putting a file or folder into the Trash is the first step in deleting it. Choosing Special⇨Empty Trash is the second and final.

Just the facts

All you need to do is choose Special⇨Empty Trash and then take a moment to check out the message that appears in the resulting dialog box. It will look something like the one shown here.

If you are confident that you know what's in the Trash and you really mean to get rid of it, click OK. Otherwise, click Cancel and double-check what's in the Trash. To do that, double-click the Trash and then look at the items in its window. If you find something you meant to keep, you can either drag it back to where it belongs, or you can click it once and choose File⇨Put Away to return it to your hard disk.

Unfortunately, you can't use the Put Away command with items that are within folders in the Trash. You either have to put away the entire folder or move the item to another location. To move an item, position the cursor over it, hold down the mouse button, and drag it to where you want to put it, and release the mouse button. The desktop works just fine for holding something while you decide what you mean to do with it.

Sometimes, your Mac refuses to obey your command to empty the Trash. When that happens, you get a message like this one.

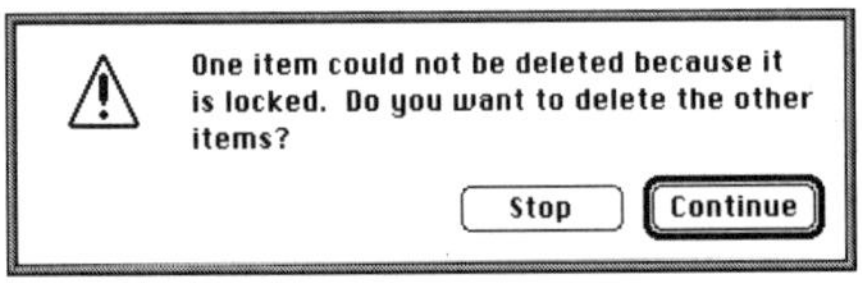

Depending upon how confident you are that you want to get rid of the files, you need to pick one of the options. If you are sure you want to get rid of the files, click Continue. If you have any doubts, click Stop.

Because a file is generally locked to deliberately prevent it from being accidentally thrown away, you may want to check that you really mean to toss out the locked file. By the way, if all of the files in the Trash are locked, your Macintosh doesn't bother counting the files or giving you a choice. It just tells you that all the files are locked and that you'll need to do something about it.

If you double-check and really do want to get rid of the locked file or files in the Trash, it's actually pretty easy to delete them. Just hold down the Option key while choosing Special⇨Empty Trash.

Sometimes, when you try to empty the Trash, your Mac tells you that it can't because the file it contains is *in use.* In other words the file is being used by a program that is currently running. You will rarely, if ever, mean to throw out a file that's in use. If you really want to delete such a file, you need to find which program is using it and either close the file, or is some cases, quit the program.

More Stuff

NOTE: When you cancel a print job, a copy of the document ends up in the Trash with the word *(print)* at the end of the filename. It's OK to go ahead and throw these files away. Your original copy of the file is OK.

REFERENCE: For information on locking files, see File⇨Get Info. For more info on the entire process of throwing out a file, see "Deleting a file" under "File Things" in Part 1.

Special⇨Erase Disk

Deletes everything from a disk and reformats it. With floppy disks, you are given a choice of which format to use.

Just the facts

Select the icon for the disk you want to erase by clicking it once. Then choose Special⇨Erase Disk. If you're erasing a floppy disk, you can choose what format to use for the disk. The dialog box with which you make this decision is shown in the following figure.

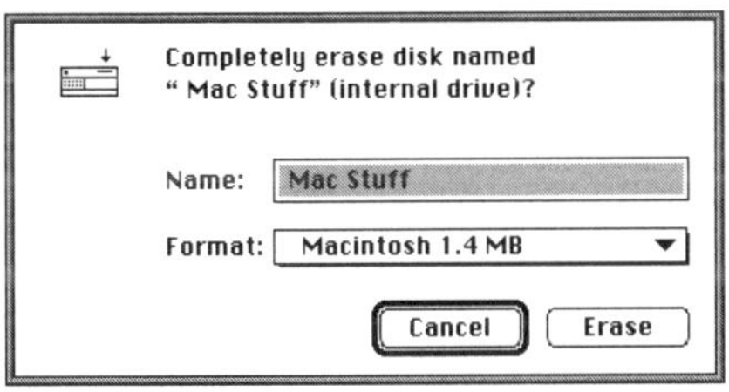

The format choices vary depending upon what type of disk you have in your disk drive. With floppy disks, you usually have several choices. Select the format you need and then decide if you want to change the name on the disk. If you do, simply type the new name. It's a good idea to do this after selecting the format so that your Macintosh can confirm that the name you picked is OK. After you make your choices, click Erase and the disk is reformatted.

If you want to reformat your hard disk, you don't need to worry about selecting a format, but you do need to be careful. Be sure that you make a copy of everything you want from your hard disk because reformatting it erases everything that is on it. And it makes sense that you can't erase your startup hard disk with this command.

More Stuff

The new process for initializing (or formatting) and erasing (or reformatting) is an improvement because it's much easier and offers more formatting choices. The only problem is that many of us are used to having several dialog boxes where you have to respond OK before the disk gets erased. With the new system, there's only one dialog box, so always read that dialog box message carefully.

If you just want to reuse a disk, double-click the disk to view what's on it and then use File⇨Select All to select everything on the disk. Next, drag all of the items into the Trash. Finally, choose Special⇨Empty Trash to throw everything out. If you want, you can change the name of the disk.

You cannot erase the disk used to start your Macintosh. (It's icon is the one in the upper-right corner of your desktop.) This restriction is a good thing because it's usually your hard disk that contains all of your important files. If you absolutely need to reformat your startup hard disk, first copy anything you want to keep to another disk. Next, use a different disk to start up your Macintosh. You will now be able to use Special⇨Erase Disk to reformat the hard disk.

Never before I have debated so much between an icon for a tip and an icon for warning. This is truly a double-headed command with both very good and very dangerous aspects. If you hold down the Option key, the ⌘ key, and the Tab key while inserting a disk, your Macintosh starts erasing the disk as soon as the disk is inserted. The advantage is it's much faster when deleting a series of disks. The disadvantage is that it makes it easier to accidentally delete a disk with something important on it. I finally decided on a tip icon because you do have one chance to decide it's all a big mistake and stop your Macintosh from erasing the disk.

Hold the disk so that the sliding metal shutter is at the bottom (pointing towards your feet) and the little metal disk in the back of the disk is facing towards you. In the upper-left corner is a little shutter that slides up-and-down. If you slide it up, the little hole is uncovered and the disk is locked — you cannot make any changes, including erasing the disk. If the shutter is closed and covering the hole, the disk is unlocked and you can make any changes you want. (By the way, if there is a hole in the upper-right corner, that means you're using what's called a *high-density* disk. It holds about twice as much as a low-density disk.)

Special⇨I'm at ...

Selects a set of PowerTalk services. When you use this command, you ensure that only those messages you want to deal with can find you. Otherwise, they are held until you reconnect to those services.

Just the facts

Because it's one of the new PowerTalk commands, Special⇨I'm at is discussed in Part 8.

Special⇨Lock Key Chain

Secures all of the PowerTalk services that you are using (such as your mailbox). This command is only available when the Key Chain is unlocked. After you lock the Key Chain, to use any of the services, you will need to enter your Access Code (password). Most services ask for the Access Code when you try to use them, but you can always use Special⇨Unlock Key Chain (which only appears when the Key Chain is locked).

Just the facts

Key Chains, PowerTalk, and other network babble is explained in Part 8.

Special⇨Restart

Shuts down your computer, making sure that all of the files are stored properly, and turns your computer off and back on again. You often need to restart your computer after installing new software or if your computer freezes or crashes (stops responding to your commands).

Just the facts

Choose Special⇨Restart and your Mac goes through the steps of the Shut Down command and then turns itself back on.

More Stuff

Although your Mac is supposed to ask you about any changes you've made to files that you haven't saved, it's still a good idea to make sure that anything you were working on is saved before choosing Special⇨Restart. After you've checked, all you do is choose the command and sit back.

Special⇨Restart does not turn off any other equipment, such as printers or scanners, that is attached to your computer. If you need to restart those components, you need to deal with each one individually. On more expensive Macs (to which you attach the monitor's power cord to the Mac), the monitor is turned on and off along with the Mac itself.

Special⇨Shut Down

Prepares your system to be turned off by doing some last minute housekeeping (making sure all of the files have been neatly put away) and then, on many Mac models, actually turns your computer off for you. On other, usually inexpensive models, you get a dialog box that tells you that it's OK to turn off the power.

Just the facts

All you really need to do is choose Special⇨Shut Down. Your Mac politely asks you about saving any changes you've made to your documents, closes all of your programs, makes sure that things are neatly stored on your disks, and ejects any disks. On many Macs, the system (including the monitor) will then turn itself off. On other Macs, you get a dialog box that says it's OK to turn off the power — you can now go ahead and flip the switch.

More Stuff

Although your Macintosh is supposed to ask you about any unsaved changes, it's often a good idea to check and make sure that you've saved any changes to your documents before shutting down. It can't hurt.

Any equipment, such as printers or scanners, attached to your Mac still needs to be turned off individually. After all, Apple has to leave you something to do. Again, on high-end Macs, the monitor will turn off at shut down if it's power cord is attached to the Mac.

One of the most popular Macintosh questions is "Why do I need to use the Shut Down command rather than just turn off my Mac?" Well, my contract prevents me from answering, but I can tell you to look in Chapter 1 of *Macintosh System 7.5 For Dummies* for the answer. Until you know the real answer, you'll just have to trust me. Always use the Shut Down command to turn off your Mac. Period.

The Apple menu⇨•Shut Down command does the same thing as the Special⇨Shut Down command. But unlike the Special⇨Shut Down command, it's available for use when you're working in programs other than the Finder.

Special⇨Unlock Key Chain

This command is the first step in making changes to your Key Chain (which is used to control what access privileges you have across the network). You only use this command if you happen to have a network and want to use it to do things other than printing.

Just the facts

The key thing to know about this command is that it's discussed in detail in Part 8.

Special⇨Visitor's Mailbox

Creates a mailbox on your desktop for someone else to use. You must be very nice to let other people get their messages at your Mac. Visitors must have a PowerTalk account somewhere on the network and a mailbox on the computer they normally use.

Just the facts

To learn more about sending and receiving mail, see Part 8.

View⇨by Comments

Displays the icons in a window as a list sorted by the information in the comments box. This command is only useful if you have added comments to the Get Info window for your files. Otherwise, all of your comments boxes are blank, and the icons are just put in alphabetical order. You control whether the by Comments command is on the View menu with the Views control panel.

Just the facts

Choose the View⇨by Comments command and see the neatly organized list.

The best way to take advantage of this command is to put information in the comments section of Get Info windows. For example, you might put the name of the project and the date the document is to be completed. If that information is in the comments box, when you choose View⇨by Comments, your list is grouped by project and sorted by due date.

More Stuff

TIP

If you want to sort a list by something other than name, you can either select the appropriate command from the View menu or click the column heading you want to use for sorting. You can only sort the information using one of the columns that's displayed in the window. If you want to use a different category of information, you have to add it to the list by using the Views control panel.

REFERENCE

Use File⇨Get Info to add comments to a file. For more information about controlling what categories of information appear within list views, see the Views control panel entry in Part 4. For information about working with the list views, see "List Things" in Part 1.

View⇨by Date

Displays the contents of the current window as a list sorted by the date on which each item was last modified. The list sorts from the most recently modified file to the file you haven't work with in a while. In other words, the files that you use most often appear at the top of the list. You control whether the by Date command is on the View menu with the Views control panel.

Just the facts

Couldn't be easier. Make sure that you're in the window that you want to work with and choose View⇨by Size. That's it. The files and folders all jump into the proper places with the most recently changed items at the top of the list.

More Stuff

TIP

To sort a list by one of the other displayed columns, simply click that column's heading in the window. You can also use the View menu to change the way the list is sorted.

For more information on controlling what categories of information appear in list views, see the entry for the Views control panel in Part 4. For information about working with the list views, see "List Things" in Part 1.

View⇨by Icon

Changes the view so that each of the files and folders is represented with an icon. The other commands on the view menu give you alternatives for displaying the same information.

Just the facts

There are two sizes of icons available. The View⇨by Icon command gives you the larger of the two (shown on the left in the following figure). To change the view to the larger icons, all you need to do is choose View⇨by Icon.

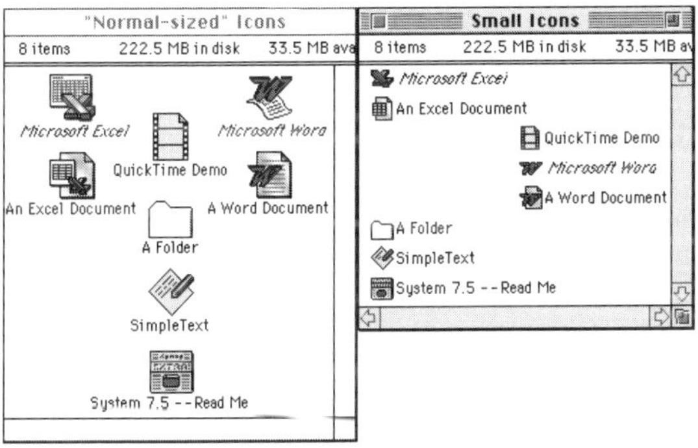

The different icons represent different types of documents and programs on your system. Most document icons look somewhat like a piece of paper with the upper-left corner folded over.

More Stuff

You control the font and size of icon names in the Finder using the Views control panel, which is discussed in Part 4. The font size of icon names affects how close together the icons are placed when you use the Special⇨Clean Up command.

To organize your icons, use Special⇨Clean Up. For more information about working with icons, see "Icon Things" in Part 1.

View⇨by Kind

Groups files by type and then puts folders at the end of the list in alphabetical order. Each file is assigned a type when it is first created. Documents you create are recognized as associated with the program you used to create them. You control whether the by Kind command is on the View menu with the Views control panel.

Just the facts

Choose View⇨by Kind and you end up with a segregated list. All of the files of each type are forced to live in their own neighborhoods. Normally, I wouldn't approve of this, but it's OK when looking for a specific type of file.

More Stuff

TIP Although the View⇨by Kind command has its uses, if you start using it often, it's time to reorganize your files. There's something wrong with your filing system if you can remember which program you used to create a file but not it's name. View⇨by Kind does come in handy when you're looking for that PowerPoint presentation on someone else's computer and you have no idea how that person names files.

TIP If you want to sort a list by something other than file type, you can either choose the appropriate command from the View menu, or you can click the column heading you want to use for sorting. You can only sort information using one of the columns displayed in the window. If you want to use a different category of information for sorting, you have to add it using the Views control panel.

REFERENCE For more information on controlling what categories of information appear in list views, see the entry for the Views control panel in Part 4. For information about working with the list views, see "List Things" in Part 1.

View⇨by Label

Displays the contents of a window as a list sorted into groups based on the label assigned to each file. View⇨by Label is really great if you use the Label menu to put your files into groups. Otherwise, it's pretty useless. You control whether the by Label command is on the View menu with the Views control panel.

Just the facts

Choose View⇨by Label and you're ready to rock and roll.

More Stuff

TIP: To change the organization of the files in your list, click another column heading, such as Date or Name. Each of the columns in your list is also represented by a menu command on the View menu.

REFERENCE: For more information on controlling what categories of information appear in list views, see the entry for the Views control panel in Part 4. For information about working with the list views, see "List Things" in Part 1.

View⇨by Name

Displays the contents of a window as a list of file names. The list is sorted alphabetically by the names of the files.

Just the facts

Choose View⇨by Name. This command is always available, and it always gives you a list sorted by the file names.

More Stuff

TIP: If you want to sort a list by something other than file names, you can either choose the appropriate command from the View menu or click the column heading you want to use for sorting. You can only sort information using one of the columns displayed in the window. If you want to use a different category of information for sorting, you have to add it using the Views control panel.

REFERENCE: For more information on controlling what categories of information appear in list views, see the entry for the Views control panel in Part 4. For information about working with the list views, see "List Things" in Part 1.

View⇨by Size

Displays the contents of the current window as a list sorted with the largest files or folders appearing first. This command may or may not be available depending on the settings of the Views control panel.

Just the facts

To organize a list so that it's sorted by size from largest to smallest, choose View➪by Size.

More Stuff

TIP Whether the Calculate folder sizes option is on in the Views control panel determines whether folders display the total size of their contents in list views. Generally, a folder and its contents are much larger than any individual file, so folders tend to appear near the top of lists sorted by size. If, however, folder's sizes aren't displayed in list views, in lists sorted by size, all of the folders appear at the end of the list sorted alphabetically.

TIP If you want to sort a list by something other than size, you can either choose the appropriate command from the View menu or click the column heading you want to use for sorting. You can only sort information using one of the columns displayed in the window. If you want to use a different category of information for sorting, you have to add it using the Views control panel.

REFERENCE For more information on controlling what categories of information appear in list views, see the entry for the Views control panel in Part 4. For information about working with the list views, see "List Things" in Part 1.

View➪by Small Icon

Changes the view so that each of the files and folders is shown as a small icon. These icons are about half the size of the ones you get when you choose View➪by Icon. The other commands on the View menu give you alternatives for displaying icons in lists.

Just the facts

It really would be difficult to make this command any easier. Pull down the View menu and choose by Small Icon.

More Stuff

TIP You control the font and size of icon names in the Finder using the Views control panel, which is discussed in Part 4. The font size of icon names affects how close together the icons are placed when you use the Special➪Clean Up command.

REFERENCE For more on working with icons, see "Icon Things" in Part 1.

View⇨by Version

Displays a list of the window's contents sorted by the version of the file. Files with small version numbers (that is, older versions) are put at the start of the list. Most document files and all folders don't have version numbers, so they're put at the bottom of the list. You can determine whether this command is even available by using the Views control panel.

Just the facts

Pull down the View menu and then choose by Version. You've got it made.

More Stuff

You'll mostly use this command to compare versions of the same file to find the newest one (which would be toward the bottom of the list). Generally, programs and their support files (such as font suitcases) have version numbers as part of their file structure. In other words, it's not easy to change version numbers, which might be a good reason to sort programs by version number rather than date if you need to find the newest one.

Sort lists by something a bit more useful by clicking one of the other column headings within the window.

For more information on controlling what categories of information appear in list views, see the entry for the Views control panel in Part 4. For information about working with the list views, see "List Things" in Part 1.

Part 3

Stop Mousing Around — Use Your Keyboard

Not all users love their mouse. In fact, there are those that absolutely hate it. No matter what your personal relationship with your mouse, there are a number of keyboard shortcuts that you can learn to save yourself time.

Working on the Desktop

All of these shortcuts work when you are viewing icons within a window. Many of them give you an alternative to pointing and clicking with the mouse. The others provide keyboards methods for ejecting discs and moving to the desktop.

Moving among icons by position

← or → or ↑ or ↓

Moving among icons alphabetically

Tab

Shift + Tab

NOTE

Tab moves you forward through the alphabet and Shift-Tab moves you backward.

Jumping to an icon by name

Start typing the first few letters of the item you want. Once you get to right part of the alphabet, you can use Tab and Shift-Tab to move between items.

Editing an item's name

Return

You have to select the item first. After you press Return, you can make any changes you want to the name. Use the left arrow and right arrow keys to move within the name.

Opening the selected item

⌘ + ↓

⌘ + O

NOTE: You can use this key combination to open a window for a selected folder, a program, or a document.

Opening the folder containing the current one

⌘ + ↑

NOTE: Imagine you have a folder name *Buried Treasure* inside a folder named *Island*. If you are working with the *Buried Treasure* folder and press ⌘-up arrow, a window showing the contents of the *Island* folder opens. If the folder you are working with is on the desktop, pressing ⌘-up arrow makes the desktop active.

Selecting the desktop

⌘ + Shift + ↑

Ejecting the selected disk temporarily

⌘ + E

Ejecting the selected disk permanently

⌘ + Y

Ejecting temporarily the disk in your first disk drive

⌘ + Shift + 1

Working with List Views

Although many true blue Macintosh users like working with list views, you can always tell the visiting PC people because it's the only view they'll ever use. These shortcuts are intended to make working with list views even easier. Almost all of the shortcuts for working with the desktop also work when you're viewing a list.

Moving through a list

↑ ↓

NOTE

You can also type the first few letters of an item's name to jump to the item, but be warned — the way your Macintosh jumps through a list with several letters will seem quite unpredictable.

Expanding the view into a folder

⌘ + →

Collapsing the view of a folder

⌘ + ←

Expanding all folders within a folder

⌘ + Option + →

Collapsing all folders within a folder

⌘ + Option + ←

Working with Any Dialog Box

It's most useful to know keyboard shortcuts when you're working with a dialog box. You often need to be typing in a name or some other information while at the same time selecting buttons or other controls within the dialog box. These shortcuts provide some useful techniques that let you keep your hands on the keyboard.

Canceling the dialog box

⌘ + .

or

Esc

Accepting the default button

Return

NOTE

Be careful with this one. Usually, pressing the default button accepts the settings and closes the dialog box, but not always. The default button has a heavy black border around it.

Jumping to an item on a list

Make sure that one of the items in the list is selected and then just start typing the first few letters of the item you want.

Moving item by item in a list

↑ ↓

NOTE

If you're working with a dialog box that has categories of settings (such as the new Print dialog box), the up and down arrow keys move you between categories.

Moving up a folder (closer to the desktop)

⌘ + ↑

Moving to the desktop

⌘ + D

Working with a Save As dialog box

It's very frustrating to be working with a Save As dialog box and find that you need to create a new folder. I always thought you had to go back to the desktop to do that, but it turns out that just isn't so. The other shortcut in this section is useful when you realize you were about to save a file in the wrong place.

Creating a new folder

⌘ + N

Moving between the name box and the list of folders

Tab

Part 4
Comfortable Customizing with Control Panels

This chapter lists many of the control panels that are included with System 7.5. For some of the control panels, I refer you to another part of this book for a complete description. I provide the control panel with a thumbs and safety rating as well as a brief description of its purpose. Most of the features in a control panel are very straightforward. If an option has a check box next to it, you can be sure that checking the box (by clicking it) will turn that option on. Clearing the box (also done by clicking it) will turn the option off. When you have a series of choices with small circles next to them, you can usually pick one of the choices, and only one, by clicking it. By the way, those little circles are called *radio buttons* and are used when only one choice in a group can be selected.

The details of working with each of the control panels, as well as suggested settings for your Macintosh, are discussed in Chapter 13 of *Macintosh System 7.5 For Dummies*. For more information about working with standard dialog boxes and controls on your Macintosh, check out *Macs For Dummies*.

Apple Menu Options

Controls whether the *submenus* for the Apple menu are on or off. You get a submenu whenever you've placed a folder, such as Control Panels or Automated Tasks, on your Apple menu. The submenu lists all of the items in the folder in a second menu that appears to the right when you highlight the folder's name. If submenus are off, you can still get to the contents of the folder by simply choosing the folder name. In fact, you can open the folder that way whether or not you are displaying the submenus.

The Apple Menu Options control panel also determines whether you see the Recent Documents, Recent Applications, and Recent Servers choices on your Apple menu. You can choose to have none of the three displayed by turning off the option that tells your Macintosh to remember recently used items. Assuming you decide that you want to display them, you can set how many items of each of the three folders displays by entering numbers in the appropriate boxes in the control panel. If you want to display some but not all of the recent categories, set the ones you don't want to display to show zero items.

The items that appear on the submenus for Recent Documents, Recent Applications, and Recent Servers are actually kept as aliases within folders within the Apple Menu Items folder.

ATM GX

The Adobe Type Manager (ATM) control panel is discussed in Part 7. The ATM GX control panel turns on Adobe Type Manager and lets you pick between preserving the line spacing in your documents (where the lines break) and maintaining the character shapes.

Auto Power On/Off

If you're one of those people who always forgets to turn the computer off when you leave the office to go home, this control panel may be the answer to all of your problems. You can use it to have your Macintosh turn itself on at a specified time (either once for a special occasion or on a regular schedule) or to have it turn itself off. There's also an option for having your Macintosh automatically restart when the power comes back following a power failure.

For more on this control panel, see "Turning the power off or on automatically" under "Desktop Things" in Part 1.

Brightness

On some Macintosh models, you can use the Brightness control panel to control your screen display and to assign a shortcut for adjusting the brightness from the keyboard. On other models, you need to use the Screen control panel (which adjusts both brightness and constrast). Most models don't use either control panel.

Button Disabler

If your Mac has physical controls on its case for the screen contrast and speaker volume and you don't want other people messing with them, you can disable the buttons with the Button Disabler control panel.

Cache Switch

Some older programs had problems with the newer processors (the 68040 series) that came out in the Centris, Quadra, and pre-Power Mac AV series. You can use the Cache Switch control panel to provide greater compatibility on those machines that need it. If this control panel isn't installed on your system, then you probably don't need it. Most people who have it use the Faster setting because very few of today's programs are incompatible with the 68040 processor.

CloseView

Magnifies a portion of the screen to make it easier to see. CloseView must be installed in your Control Panels folder when your Mac starts up in order for it to work. If you add the CloseView control panel later, you need to restart your Mac to make the features available.

If the CloseView control panel is in your Control Panels folder, you can turn the control panel on or off by holding down the Option key and pressing ⌘-O. When CloseView is on, the area to be magnified is enclosed by a heavy black border.

Once CloseView has been turned on, you can activate the magnfication by holding down the Option key and pressing ⌘-X. To adjust the magnification, hold down the Option key and the ⌘ key and press the up arrow or the down arrow.

REFERENCE: The Easy Access control panel is another utility that makes System 7.5 even easier to use.

Color

Use the Color control panel to select which color is used when highlighting text and which color is used for the shading on the window title bar. Truly compulsive people use this control panel every morning to coordinate their Mac with their outfit.

ColorSync System Profile

NEW 7.5

This control panel's sole purpose is to let you pick a *color profile* for your current monitor. A color profile is used to provide programs with information about the colors available on your monitor so that the colors in your documents are displayed and printed as accurately as possible.

CPU Energy Saver

NEW 7.5

Serves the same purpose as your parents — it turns lights off after you leave the room. With this control panel, you can set your Mac to turn itself off after a specific amount of idle time or shut down at a specific time. There are even options for setting what sort of events will prevent a system shut down. The only bad thing about this control panel is that the shut down countdown is more appropriate for a nuclear attack than a friendly computer.

WARNING!

There's one major problem with the CPU Energy Saver on some Macs — it forgets its settings every time you turn off your computer. That means that each time you start up, you have to reset the shut down. This bug is quite annoying, and we all know that Apple, with its wonderful reputation for customer support, will get it fixed real soon.

Date & Time

Not only can you set the correct date and time, but there are buttons for setting the Date Formats and Time Formats as well. You can also select your current time zone by selecting a city within the same time zone. (Unless you live in a big enough city to make it on the list, in which case you can just select the city you're in.) Finally, Apple buried within this control panel all of the settings for the menu bar clock. Clicking the Clock Options button opens an entire dialog box with settings for displaying the time. You can even set this control panel so that you have a chiming clock.

Desktop Patterns

NEW 7.5

Gone are the boring desktop patterns of previous systems. The new patterns are larger and much more elaborate. Unfortunately, also gone is the ability to edit the desktop pattern yourself. You will, however, be able to copy patterns from other sources and paste them into the control panel. When you find a pattern you like, just click the top Set Desktop Pattern button to use it as your background for your desktop. (For those who care about such things, Desktop Patterns isn't really a control panel — it's a little bitty program that Apple put in the Control Panels folder.)

Easy Access

The Easy Access control panel must be in your Control Panels folder when your computer starts before you can use any of the features. If you move to the Control Panels folder while your system is running, you'll need to restart your Mac.

Each of the Easy Access features simplifies some aspect of using the mouse or keyboard. Mouse Keys lets you use the numeric keypad in place of the mouse. Slow Key tells your Mac to wait a little longer before accepting a keystroke, which means that you have to hold down each key a bit longer before it is recognized. This feature is very useful if you cannot avoid hitting extra keys when reaching for the key you need and you want your Mac to ignore those extra keystrokes.

Sticky Keys lets you push key combinations in sequences rather than together; you should use it if you cannot hold down more than a single key. With Sticky Keys activated, rather than holding down the Option key and the ⌘ key and pressing the letter O, you can press the Option key and release it, press the ⌘ key and release it, and then press the letter O and release it.

WARNING!

If Easy Access is in your Control Panels folder when you start your Mac, you can turn on the features by using keyboard shortcuts. I use the warning icon because many users turn on Easy Access by accident while typing. Fortunately, as long as the audio feedback is turned on, you'll hear a tone to warn you that an Easy Access feature has been turned on or off. You then have to figure out why your Mac is making funny noises.

TIP

Turn on Sticky Keys by pressing the Shift key five times in a row. Turn it off by holding down the ⌘, Option, and Shift keys. Slow Keys turns on if you hold the Return key down for a long time (about 10 seconds). You turn it off in the same way. ⌘+Shift+Clear turns Mouse Keys on or off.

Energy Saver

You can control whether the screen turns itself off after a fixed amount of time and set how long that amount of time is. When your screen is off and you move the mouse to wake it up, it may take a moment. If so, your system will just beep at you while it refreshes the screen.

NOTE

This control panel is not included with System 7.5 but is found on many machines that have upgraded from previous versions of the system.

Extension Manager

REFERENCE

The Extension Manager control panel is discussed in Part 5, which is devoted solely to extensions. This control panel controls which extensions and control panels are loaded when you start up your Macintosh.

File Sharing Monitor

REFERENCE

The File Sharing Monitor control panel is discussed in Part 8. You use this control panel to monitor what volumes on your Mac are being shared and who is connected to your Macintosh across a network. You can also use it to disconnect users if you need to.

General Controls

You know that kitchen drawer you have? You know, the one with all the odds and ends you've slipped into it. Well, this is the control panel equivalent. If an option didn't fit on another control panel and wasn't worth a control panel of its own, it shows up under General Controls.

In the upper-right corner, you have two sections that control how fast things blink. The insertion point is the location where text that you type will be inserted. Menu blinking is the phenomena that occurs when you let up on the mouse button after choosing a command.

Some of the other features floating around in the General Controls include options for protecting your System Folder or an Applications folder. This protection feature is not available when file sharing is on. You can also ask to be notified if the computer is shut down improperly.

One of the most far-reaching options is down in the lower-left corner. Previously, programs almost always assumed that the first time that you opened a file or saved a file, you wanted to put the file in the same folder as the program. Now, you have the option of telling the program what to assume. In fact, you can create a Documents folder and tell other programs to default to this folder.

The upper-left corner of the General Controls control panel has two totally different options grouped together in the Desktop area. You can control whether you see the Desktop icons in the background when you're working with another program, and you can control whether the Launcher program is automatically opened when you start up your computer. To find out more about Launcher, check out the Launcher control panel in this chapter. Hiding the desktop is discussed in Part 1.

Keyboard

Do you ever find yourself getting thirteen *S*s when you only wanted one? If so, the Keyboard control panel is for you. You can set how long the system waits before it starts repeating and how quickly it repeats after it starts. You can also select what style of keyboard your computer is using. To see the results of changing the keyboard layout check out Apple menu⇨Key Caps.

Labels

If you've ever wondered where the information on the Labels menu comes from, look no further. You can change the text for each label and, if you double-click the color sample, the colors as well. Changing the colors is fun because there are two separate systems available for picking colors. (If you only see one after double-clicking the color sample, click the More Choices button.) I like trying to create interesting color combinations. Hey, it beats writing.

Launcher

The Launcher control panel isn't really a control panel at all. It's actually the command to start Launcher. Launcher is a very simple utility that offers an alternative to searching through your folders to find the program you want. Instead, you get the Launcher window which contains large buttons, one for each program or document you've installed. To install a program or document in the Launcher window, put an alias of it into the Launcher Items folder (found within the System Folder). If you decide you really like using Launcher, you can have it automatically open when you start your Macintosh by using the General Controls control panel.

Macintosh Easy Open

Macintosh Easy Open is one of two control panels that makes it easy to use files created on non-Macintosh computers. (The other is PC Exchange.) Macintosh Easy Open is responsible for suggesting application programs for documents for which you don't have the true creator application. If you have a document that was created by a program on your Macintosh, double-clicking that document opens the program. If you double-click a document created by a program that you don't have on your Macintosh, Macintosh Easy Open comes into play and suggests other programs that might be able to open the document. You can decide whether you want your Macintosh to automatically try a program if there's only one choice and whether your Macintosh should consider programs that are located on the network in addition to your hard disk(s).

MacTCP

Lets your Mac connect to a UNIX-based network. This is one of the very few control panels that is really a nerds-only feature. In order to use it, you have to have installed the hardware necessary to communicate with the other computer system. Whoever did that should also set the features on this control panel. Maybe that's why you have to install this one by hand from the System 7.5 Installer's Custom Install option. You'll find it under Networking after you choose the Custom Install option.

Map

The Map control panel tells you the location, time zone, and current time for any city in its database. For cities big enough to be included in the Map database, you can use Map to find the distance to any other city in the database. (Use the Set button to indicate that the current city is your hometown and the location from which you wish to measure distances.) If you live in a smaller city, you can add your town to the database if you find out the latitude and longitude. You can find out what cities are in the database by checking the time zones in the Date & Time control panel. If that idea appeals to you, get a life.

Memory

CROSS-REFERENCE FOR DUMMIES

This isn't anything that Barbara Streisand would be singing about. Fortunately, it is something that other authors are willing to write about. For more information on all of the exciting things that can be done to configure the way your Macintosh uses memory, see Chapter 10 of *Macintosh System 7.5 For Dummies*.

Monitors

If you have more than one monitor, you can use the Monitors control panel to determine which parts of the screen appears on which monitor. Even with only one monitor, you can use this control panel to choose the number of colors or grays displayed on-screen.

Mouse

The Mouse control panel sets how fast you have to double-click and how far you have to move the mouse to move the cursor on-screen. The second control is often called the mouse tracking speed.

Network

REFERENCE

The Network control panel is discussed in Part 8. You use the Network control panel to select what type of network technology you are using.

Numbers

Your programs need to know what sort of format to use for numbers. Some programs have a format built in, but others look to the Numbers control panel for the answer. You can set the symbols used for separating the parts of the number as well as the symbol and its position for a currency format.

PC Exchange

PC Exchange, along with Macintosh Easy Open, makes it easy to use disks formatted on non-Macintosh computers. Macintosh Easy Open enables your Mac to suggest programs for documents that it otherwise could not open. PC Exchange lets your Mac recognize disks from DOS, Windows, or the Apple II. With it, you can assign a specific program to a document that was created on a DOS or Windows machine. With PC Exchange, your Mac looks at the file extension (the part of the DOS file name following the required period) and uses the extension to determine which program will open the document. You use the PC Exchange control panel to assign programs to specific extensions.

Power Macintosh Card

Controls whether your Power Macintosh Card is turned on when you start up your computer. If you don't have a Power Macintosh Card, then this control panel won't do you any good. Wouldn't it be great if they designed a control panel that upgraded your Mac to a new PowerMac? Unfortunately, those Power Macintosh Cards actually cost a fair bit.

PowerTalk Setup

The PowerTalk Setup control panel controls the use of your Key Chain and is discussed in Part 8 (which is also where Key Chains are explained).

Screen

Controls the brightness and contrast for certain Macintosh monitors and enables you to turn off the built-in screen to conserve power. You set the length of time that the system must be inactive before the screen is turned off. Other Macintosh models may use the Brightness control panel for a similar purpose. To turn your external monitor off automatically, you should look for the Energy Saver control panel.

Serial Switch

On Macs whose serial port is of the new, high-speed, fancy variety, you may need to use the Serial Switch control panel to choose between the faster performance and improved compatibility.

Sharing Setup

The Sharing Setup control panel is discussed in Part 8. You use this control panel to give your Mac a network identity.

Sound

Not only can you control which sound is used for the alert (the System beep), but you can now control the volume for different speakers or headphones and change options for both the input and output devices.

Startup Disk

Well, if you have more than one hard disk, this control panel is very important because it tells your Mac which volume to check first for a System Folder when starting up. If you only have one hard disk, this control panel is sort of useless, though you probably shouldn't throw it away. After all, maybe someone will buy you a new hard disk for your birthday, and if you have enough RAM for it, you may decide to boot from a RAM disk once in a while.

Text

NEW 7.5

The Text control panel lets you change the alphabet used for sorting information (the Behavior) and how text is organized on your screen (the Script). These options are particularly useful if you use more than one language in your writing and absolutely crucial if the languages you use are read in different directions (for example, Hebrew reads right to left while English reads left to right).

User & Groups

REFERENCE

The User & Groups control panel is discussed in Part 8 and is used to determine who is allowed to use files on your Mac once it's connected to a network.

Views

You can choose between having a straight grid or a staggered grid and whether, when you move an item, it snaps to position on the grid. You can also select which items of information appear in the list views and on the View menu. One of the less-know features is the capability to choose which font is used for the names of icons in the Finder. Changing the font changes the size of the names, which in turn changes the spacing for the grid. The last two options on the control panel are used to determine whether the size is calculated for folders and whether the available disk space is shown at the top of each window when you are using list views.

NOTE

To temporarily switch the setting for snap to grid, hold down the ⌘ key while dragging an item.

REFERENCE

To find out more about using the various views, see "Icons Things" and "List Things" in Part 1.

WindowShade

NEW 7.5

The WindowShade feature is, in my opinion, the absolute coolest thing in System 7.5 and well worth the upgrade. You use the control panel to set what you have to do to roll window shades up or down. You can also use it to turn off the WindowShade feature, but who would want to do that? The whooshing sound alone is worth keeping it on.

REFERENCE

To find out how to use the WindowShade feature, see "Rolling up the window shade" under "Window Things" in Part 1.

Part 5

Puzzling Out the Extensions

They used to be called INITs, but now they're just extensions. These files are stored in the Extensions folder within the System Folder and add functionality to your Macintosh. Basically, an extension adds at startup a function or feature that isn't built into the System file or Finder. This chapter lists the standard extensions that come with System 7.5 and, where possible, points you to where you can find out more about the services provided by that extension.

The most important thing to know about extensions is that they load at startup immediately following the main files for the System 7.5 and before the Finder desktop appears. Because extensions load before your Mac presents you with the Finder, if you have two extensions that don't get along, your Mac may not start up correctly. By the way, *loading* refers to when a file is read from disk (storage) into RAM (working memory).

Extensions aren't the only things that load as your system starts. Many control panels and some other special files also load at that time. If you watch as your Mac starts up, you'll see icons appearing across the bottom of your screen. These icons represent some of the extensions and control panels as they load. You can use the figures in this chapter and those in Part 4 to identify those control panels and extensions that are a part of System 7.5. If your system freezes while extensions and control panels are loading and refuses to continue to start up, try turning off whichever extension or control panel appeared last.

TIP

By the way, every Mac user should know that you can start up without any extensions or control panels loading by holding down the Shift key during the startup process. When you turn on your Mac, press and hold the Shift key until the *Extensions off* message appears on-screen. Why would you want to start up without extensions? There are several reasons. If an extension causes your Mac to crash at startup, then starting up without extensions allows you to get your Mac up and running (albeit without the functionality of all your extensions and control panels) so that you can correct what's causing the problem.

NOTE

If you start up without extensions, your Mac won't have many of the features you know and love. You won't be able to print or use a network; your Apple menu won't have submenus; you won't be able to play CDs; and, needless to say, none of your third-party extensions or control panels will work.

NEW 7.5

You can use the Extensions Manager control panel to decide which of your extensions load. Of course, Apple realized that if you have problems starting your Mac, you need a way to get to the Extensions Manager. The secret is to hold down the spacebar while starting your Mac. After loading the very basics of System 7.5, but before any of the extensions or control panels, the

Extensions Manager appears on your screen so that you can select which items to load.

In addition to extensions, which add features to your system, the Extensions folder also includes special files required for printing, faxing, and network access. These files are actually called *Chooser extensions* because you often configure them using the Chooser (accessed via the Apple menu). I don't discuss Chooser extensions in this part of the book because the ones you use on your system depend on the kind of printer, modem, fax machine, or network you have installed. A bit more information about printer Chooser extensions is presented in Part 7.

Generally speaking, there are only two times when you want to remove an extension from a system folder. One is if the extension is causing problems. You can be fairly confident that the extensions listed here are not going to be the ones to blame if you have a startup problem. The other reason to remove an extension is to free up memory or disk storage space. For information on the RAM and disk space requirements of just about every extension and control panel, and for information on the consequences of disabling or removing these items, see Chapter 15 of *Macintosh System 7.5 For Dummies*.

Extensions Manager Control Panel

Why, you might well ask, is the first entry in a chapter on extensions about a control panel? Well, the answer is quite simple. The Extensions Manager control panel is a long overdue tool for selectively loading your extensions. When you open this control panel, you see a list of all of the extensions that are in your System Folder plus any control panels or other files that load as your system starts up. Those that will load the next time you start up your Mac are marked with a check. If you suspect that a particular file is causing problems, you can click the file to remove the check mark and thus prevent it from loading the next time you start up your Mac.

Another useful feature is that you can store sets of extensions, which allows you to easily switch between groups of extensions. So, for example, if you only use QuickTime on rare occasions, you can store two sets, one with QuickTime and one without. That way, you can start up with QuickTime only when you know you'll need it. Apple provides a built-in set, called System 7.5 Only, for loading just those extensions and control panels that are part of System 7.5.

As mentioned in the introduction to this part, you can prevent any extensions from loading as your Macintosh starts by holding down the Shift key as you start your system. Alternatively, you can hold down the spacebar to have your Mac display the Extensions Manager before it loads any extensions or control panels. If you hold down the spacebar, you can use the Extensions Manager to choose a set of extensions to load, or you can selectively enable or disable your extensions and control panels.

The EM Extension appears at the start of any alphabetical list of extension names because Apple put a space at the start of its name. This extension has to be loaded (preferably first, which is the reason for the space at the start of its name) in order for the Extensions Manager to work.

Apple Event Manager

Apple Event Manager allows your Mac to recognize new types of events and coordinate these events with scripting language. An event can be as simple as a mouse click or as complex as the behavior of a program. Scripting is a technology used to record series of instructions for your Mac to perform. For more on scripting, see Part 6.

Apple CD-ROM

This extension enables your Mac to communicate with a particular device — in this case, an Apple CD-ROM drive.

Apple Guide

The Apple Guide technology is Apple's new help system. It's available throughout System 7.5 and in newer programs for the Macintosh. This extension is the heart of Apple Guide. Without it in your Extensions folder, you will not be able to access any of the Guides.

The Apple Guide document icon is used for document files that contain the information for the Guides. Calling them documents is a little misleading because you cannot open them like normal documents. If you double-click one of them, you get a message reminding you that a Guide can only be run within the application that it is associated with. Also, unlike most files on your Macintosh, it very much matters where the Guide document is located. Guides that come with System 7.5 (About Apple Guide, Macintosh Guide, Tutorial, Shortcuts, and PowerTalk Guide) must remain in the Extensions folder if you want to use them. In general, you shouldn't move the Guides once they are installed (if you plan on using them).

The Apple Guide Additions icon marks extensions that add more features to Apple Guide. For example, System 7.5 stores two additions in your Extensions folder: one for adding speech to a Guide and another that allows a Guide to contain video clips. In general, these additions to the Guide technology belong in your Extensions folder.

Apple Photo Access

You need this extension in order to display the images from a Kodak Photo CD on your Mac.

AppleScript

NEW 7.5

AppleScript is a technology that allows you to record a series of instructions for your Macintosh to perform upon command. Within a program, this functionality is usually referred to as a *macro language*, but when it works throughout a system, this kind of feature has a variety of different names. In DOS (ick!), it's called *batch file programming*; in UNIX, it's called *shell programming*; and on your Macintosh, it's called *scripting*.

There are a couple of different files associated with the scripting technology, but all of them show a blank document for their icon so it would be boring to include them. If an extension's name contains the word *script*, it probably is part of the scripting technology. (Finder Scripting Extension has its own puzzle piece icon, so it got an entry of its own.)

You'll also find a folder in the Extensions folder called Scripting Additions. It has extensions to the scripting technology which are identified with an icon that looks like a scroll with a small puzzle piece added. There are also dialect files which have an icon of a scroll with a small world attached.

REFERENCE

The scripting language is introduced in Part 6.

AppleShare

AppleShare is actually a Chooser extension, but it has only a little to do with printing. It allows you to use an AppleTalk network to communicate with other computers or with printers. You need this extension to use your Apple network with or without PowerTalk. For more about Apple's network technology, see Part 8.

AppleTalk Services

This is a PowerTalk extension that provides the necessary components for communicating across an AppleTalk network. For more information, see Part 8.

Catalogs Extension

The whole concept of catalogs, which are what this extension provides, is discussed in Part 8. This is one of the extensions managed by the PowerTalk Manager extension.

Clipping Extension

A *clipping* is a file that contains information to be inserted into another file. Previously, you moved information by putting it on the Clipboard. Now, you can put the information into a clippings file. To find out the basics about using a clipping, see "Using desktop clippings" under "Desktop Things" in Part 1.

Color Picker

NEW 7.5

Would you be surprised if I told you that this extension helps you pick colors? Well, actually, the Color Picker gives you several ways to pick colors. For an example of this extension in action, choose Apple menu⇨Control Panels⇨Color. From the Highlight color pop-up menu, choose the

Other option. With the Color Picker extension installed, the new and improved Color Picker appears. For those of you who have used the old method for picking colors, you'll immediately notice a change for the better. For those new to Mac System software, trust me: the new Color Picker is much better than the one you'd get if you didn't have the Color Picker extension. Play around with it for a while; maybe choose a highlight color for yourself. When you're done, click OK. (To see the old color-picking system, restart your Mac without the Color Picker extension.)

ColorSync

This is the extension that makes the ColorSync control panel actually work. The ColorSync technology helps calibrate the way your monitor displays colors so that what you see is consistent with input from color scanners and output to color printers.

EtherTalk Phase 2

EtherTalk is the high-speed network technology that is used on EtherNet cabling. It's much faster than AppleTalk but provides the same basic services. You need this extension to use an EtherTalk network with or without PowerTalk. What you might use a network for is discussed in Part 8.

File Sharing Extension

This extension enables you to share files across a network with or without PowerTalk. Some of the basics of file sharing are covered in Part 8.

For all the ins and outs of file sharing, see Chapter 9 of *Macintosh System 7.5 For Dummies.*

Find File Extension

The new, improved Find File is available as Apple⇨Find File and File⇨Find. It's covered in Part 2 under File⇨Find. If you want to permanently use the old Find File available in previous versions of the system, you need to remove this extension from the Extensions folder.

Finder Help

The little balloon on the face of this extension provides a clue to its purpose. This extension contains the information for the help balloons that appear when you turn on balloon help in the Finder. You turn balloon help on by choosing ?⇨Show Balloons; you turn balloons off by choosing ?⇨Hide Balloons.

Finder Scripting Extension

Provides the portion of the scripting technology that is used when writing scripts involving commands in the Finder. For more information about scripting, see Part 6.

Foreign File Access

This extension allows you to extend the types of file system formats that your Mac can recognize. The use of this extension is primarily restricted to CD formats.

Mailbox Extension

One of several extensions that provides PowerTalk services. This one is responsible for maintaining your mailbox and communicating with mail services. For more information about PowerTalk services, see Part 8. This is one of the extensions managed by the PowerTalk Manager extension.

?? Monitors Extension

Replace the question marks in entry above with the name of your Mac's series (such as *PowerBook* Monitors Extension or *Quadra AV* Monitors Extension). This extension provides some of the options in the Monitors control panel. The type of options you get depend on the kind of Mac you're using (hence the several variations of this extension).

Network Extension

This extension adds network communications technology to your Macintosh. For a better idea of what I mean by network communications technology, see Part 8. (Network communication technology is one of those phrases invented by somebody who is paid by the syllable.)

PDD Maker GX

When is a printer definition not a printer definition? When it's designed for creating portable documents. A portable document is one that can be read on any Macintosh, regardless of what fonts or programs are available. For more information on portable documents, see the section on them in Part 7.

PowerPC Finder Update

Would you believe it adds some information to update the Finder's code for Power Mac? Well, it does. Obviously, you probably don't need this one unless you have a Power Mac.

PowerTalk Extension

Not surprisingly, this is the extension that provides the basis for using PowerTalk on your Macintosh. For more information on the benefits of PowerTalk, see Part 8.

PowerTalk Manager

If you look closely at the icon, you might get an idea of what this extension is used for. It manages the PowerTalk services provided by other extensions such as the Catalogs Extension and the Mailbox Extension. For more information about these PowerTalk services, see Part 8.

Printer Share

Enables the use of such devices as plotters across a network.

Printer Share GX

Similar to the Printer Share extension, this one also enables the use of devices such as plotters across a network, but you use the GX version of this extension if you've installed QuickDraw GX.

PrintMonitor

This so-called extension is actually a program. It gives you the option of printing in the background while doing something else on your Mac (if you aren't using QuickDraw GX). The temporary files used by the PrintMonitor are stored in a folder called PrintMonitor Documents. For more information on using PrintMonitor, see the section on printing without QuickDraw GX in Part 7.

QuickDraw GX

This is it! The extension you've heard so much about — QuickDraw GX. Having this extension on your system means that you've chosen to join the elite group of those using the new printing technology. Of course, I guess it could mean that somebody else decided that you were going to use the new technology even if you really didn't want to. To find out more about what QuickDraw GX does for you (and *to* you), see Part 7.

QuickTime

QuickTime is becoming an industry standard for displaying multimedia information. Its primary purpose is to control the display of audio and video clips. This extension adds the QuickTime technology to your Macintosh.

QuickTime PowerPlug

Additional QuickTime technology that controls the display of sound and video clips in multimedia material on your Macintosh.

SCSI Manager 4.3

SCSI is one of my favorite acronyms. After all, which would you rather say, *scuzzy* (the way it's normally said) or *Small Computer System Interface* (what it stands for)? You probably have at least one device connected to your Macintosh using SCSI technology — your hard disk. In addition, some printers are connected this way. CD-ROM drives, scanners, and most storage devices for the Mac use SCSI. This extension improves the performance of devices whose drivers are compatible with it. Some are; some aren't. You'll have to contact the manufacturers of your SCSI devices to determine whether they're compatible with SCSI Manager 4.3. If so, keep the extension. If not, either trash this extension or see if the manufacturer will send you (for free or for a tiny fee) an updated version of the driver required for your SCSI device. Most new SCSI devices are compatible with SCSI Manager 4.3.

Part 6

Acting Lessons: Using Scripts

If you've ever found yourself doing the same series of steps over and over, then you've discovered the reason that System 7.5 now contains *scripts*. A script is a series of instructions that you store as a program so that your Mac can perform the instructions upon your command. Create a script once and you can repeat the actions as many times as you wish. For example, you might write a script that creates an alias for a file, puts that alias in the Apple Menu Items folder, and removes the word *alias* from the end of the file name. (Actually, you wouldn't have to write this script because Apple's already written it for you, and it's called Add Alias to Apple Menu.)

Running a script is as easy as running any program. You can double-click the icon that represents the script or, if the script is in the Apple Menu Items folder, you can select the script from a menu. When you are running scripts, you should be aware of the difference between the two most common forms of scripts. As with most things on your Mac, the difference shows up in the script's icons.

Scripts with this icon perform a task on your Mac which probably doesn't involve any specific files. The script might turn a particular feature on or off, or the script might open several programs and arrange the windows the way you like to work with them.

Scripts with this icon are expecting you to select a group of files for the script to use. There are two ways for you to tell the script which files to use.

- Select the items you want the script to use and then start the script normally (by double-clicking it or by choosing it from a menu).
- Select the files and drag them onto the script's icon.

Scripting is a relatively new technology, and all the problems haven't been ironed out in its implementation in System 7.5. Some of the scripts included with System 7.5 have minor problems that you may run into when you try to use them. Apple has done everything possible to ensure that even if one of their scripts doesn't do what it's supposed to do, at least it won't hurt your system.

If you've worked with a spreadsheet program, you may be thinking, "What's the difference between a script and a macro?" Well, the only difference is that different people named them. They both serve the exact same purpose.

With System 7.5, scripts are created using the AppleScript *scripting language* — special instructions with their own vocabulary and syntax. In order for a script to work within a program, the program needs to be *scriptable* (that's Apple-speak). Basically, the program needs to know how to communicate with Apple Script; otherwise, your script won't be able to work with the program. As you would expect, the Finder that comes with System 7.5 is scriptable.

Well, all of this technology sounds very interesting (at least I hope it does), but where do you get scripts? A few are included with System 7.5. You can find these scripts in the Automated Tasks folder on the Apple menu. You can also create your own scripts either by recording them or by writing them. The problem with creating your own scripts is that you must be very precise in the instructions you give. Your Mac will do exactly what the script says, not what you meant. In fact, the dreaded secret of creating your own scripts is that it's actually a type of programming. (At this point, the typical Mac user should gasp in horror. Unlike users of Windows and DOS computers, a Mac user can go for years without typing a single command, let alone do any programming.)

TIP

If you are interested in learning how to create your own scripts, there are a couple of good places to start. You should take a look at the files that come with System 7.5 (Using AppleScript part 1 and Using AppleScript part 2). You can also use the Script Editor (which is included with System 7.5) to look at the scripts Apple provided. Oddly enough, several of the scripts in the More Automated Tasks folder are a bit easier to understand. You can also use the Script Editor to record your actions and then use its recording as the basis for your script. Examining those scripts will help you learn how your Mac records in AppleScript.

I expect that scripts will become hot items as *shareware.* Shareware programs are available through bulletin boards, online services, and user groups. Authors of this kind of software put their products where the public can access them and give them a try. Those who decide that they like a particular piece of shareware are expected to pay the author's requested fee. Generally, shareware fees range from $10 to $50, which is less than what you would pay for most shrink-wrapped software at stores. Programs distributed without a fee are called *freeware*.

WARNING!

The only problem with shareware scripts becoming popular is the risk of viruses. (A *virus* is a program that can copy itself from one disk to another and start making changes to your system without you even being aware of the changes.) Whenever you run shareware or freeware on your computer, be sure to practice *safe computing*. Don't take disks from a stranger. Don't put anything into your disk drive unless you know where it's been. Be suspicious of offers that sound too good to be true. Any program can spread a virus. Generally speaking, documents cannot. Keep in mind that scripts, although they are smaller and are created with the Script Editor, are in fact programs. If you frequent bulletin boards or on-line services, get yourself some virus protection software.

For a description of the scripts provided with System 7.5, see *Macintosh System 7.5 For Dummies.*

Part 7

Printing Perfection

Printing is such a difficult subject to talk about. It's not that I have a lot of emotional issues over putting words to paper, but the subject can be so complex. Those of us who remember the very early Macintoshes know that one of the most impressive features was the quality of the printed output. The Mac still has the best print quality around, but the process of printing has gotten more complex.

For starters, your Mac displays different Print and Page Setup dialog boxes to match your printer. So, if you use an ImageWriter, you get dialog boxes that are different from the ones used by LaserWriters. The following two figures show the Page Setup dialog boxes for an ImageWriter and for a Personal LaserWriter SC. Notice the variety of different options available for the two kinds of printers.

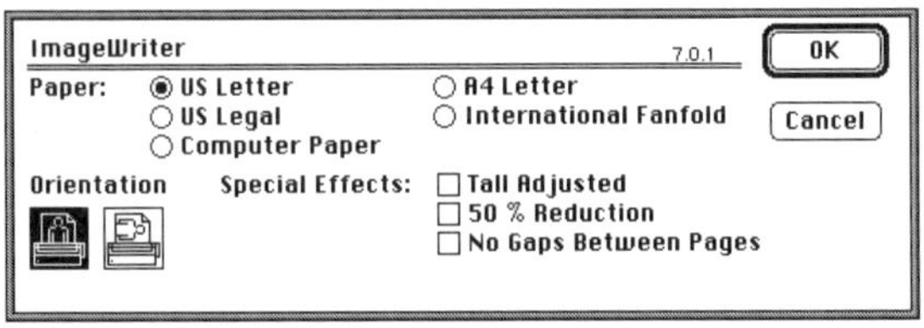

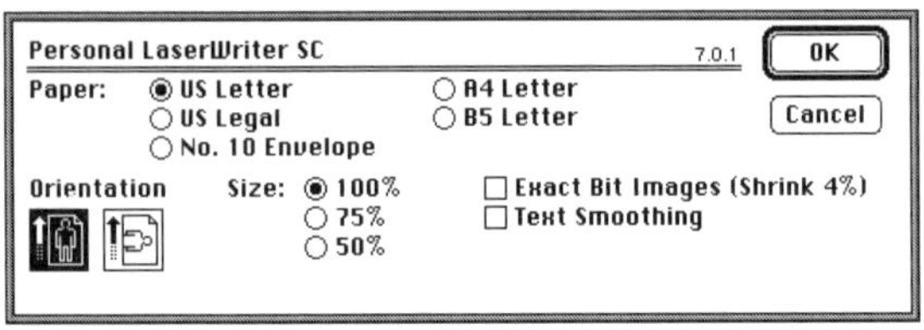

Because each printer can have its own Print and Page Setup dialog boxes, and because many programs add their own options to both kinds of dialog boxes, I could quite easily fill an entire book describing the options available in every Print and Page Setup dialog box. Because this book is not titled *Macintosh Printing For Dummies Quick Reference*, you're not going to get that kind of coverage. To give you the information you need without boring you with discussions of twenty-seven other printers, I've tried to keep the discussion general and used the LaserWriter dialog boxes for most of the figures, but there are a few exceptions.

NOTE

I haven't forgotten that many people don't have Apple printers, and I realize that some of those printers, such as fax modems, don't even print to paper. If you run into hardware or software problems with non-Apple products, you best bet is to check your owner's manual or contact the manufacturer.

NEW 7.5

To add to the complexity, with System 7.5, printing can take on a whole new look — at least for some people. I'm talking about *QuickDraw GX*. QuickDraw is the part of your system software and is used for drawing images on-screen. It also helps facilitate communication with your printer. QuickDraw GX is a new, much improved version of QuickDraw. It changes the way your Macintosh goes about printing documents, and it adds a number of powerful features, including portable documents. On the plus side, QuickDraw GX uses standard Page Setup and Print dialog boxes that are shared by all printers. On the down side, you have to learn about such things as *desktop printers*, and you'll also have to learn a few new ways of doing things.

CROSS-REFERENCE

To find out more about the actual QuickDraw GX technology, you should take a look at Chapter 8 of *Macintosh System 7.5 For Dummies*.

The rest of this part is broken into three sections — "Printing without QuickDraw GX," "Printing with QuickDraw GX," and "Portable Documents." If you didn't install QuickDraw GX, the explanations for the commands you use are discussed in the first section. If you did install QuickDraw GX, the second section contains the explanations you need, including information about the ATM GX and ColorSync control panels. The final section, "Portable Documents," assumes you've installed QuickDraw GX and that you want to create electronic documents that can be read on someone else's system — even if the other system doesn't have the program or the fonts that you used to create the document.

Printing without QuickDraw GX

If you didn't install QuickDraw GX, you'll find that printing hasn't changed all that much from previous versions of System 7. You use Apple menu⇨Chooser to choose which printer to use and the Print and Page Setup commands from the File menu to actually control printing. If you are using background printing, printing is actually a two-step process. Your program prints to PrintMonitor, and PrintMonitor sends the document to the printer. Background printing lets you continue to work with your programs while your document prints. This section starts by describing some of the very basic printing tasks and concludes with a list of the commands that you need to know.

Installing a printer

To let your Mac know that there's a printer out there, you need to have the appropriate printer driver in your Extensions folder. The printer driver should have the same name as your printer model (for example, StyleWriter). If your printer was manufactured by Apple, the printer file you need was probably already installed in your System folder when you upgraded to System 7.5, and you shouldn't need to do anything else. Non-Apple printers should include a disk with the printer driver for your printer. If not, try to get a copy from whomever sold you the printer. Once you've located the printer driver, drag a copy of it into your System Folder (where it should be automatically placed in the Extensions folder). Assuming you've connected the printer's cables correctly, you should now be able to set up your printer.

Setting up a printer

After installing a new printer or upgrading an existing printer to System 7.5, you may need to configure the printer file to work with your specific printer model. Choose Apple menu⇨Chooser and select your printer. (Apple menu⇨Chooser is discussed later in this chapter.) If there is a Setup button in the bottom portion of the screen, go ahead and click it. If the button says Review, then you only need to click it if you've made some change to your printer. You may get a second dialog box with another Setup button. If so, click that one too. That's it. Your printer's been installed.

Using background printing

Many printers, including most of those made by Apple (except for the ImageWriter), let you continue working on your Macintosh while PrintMonitor prints your document for you. This feature is called *background printing*. If you find that your computer works too sluggishly while printing to be of any use, you probably want to turn off the background printing feature.

To check whether your printer uses background printing, and to change whether it's on or off, choose Apple menu⇨Chooser and then click the printer you want to use. If your printer uses background printing, you'll see an option in the lower-right corner (above the buttons for turning AppleTalk on or off). If your printer doesn't use background printing, that area may be blank, or it may contain a Setup button. Background printing has only two buttons, and you can only select one of them, so it's a simple of matter of clicking either the On or Off button. With background printing turned on, the documents you print are sent to the PrintMonitor, and the PrintMonitor takes care of communicating with your printer so that the programs you're using don't have to. That way, you can get back to work. With background printing turned off, the documents you print are sent directly to the printer and you have to wait until they're done printing before you can return to work.

Printing from the desktop

To print a document or documents from the desktop, first highlight the document or documents and then choose File⇨Print. Your Mac opens the program that created the document and displays that program's Print dialog box. Alter the settings if you like and then click Print. If you are printing more than one document, you may have to complete a Print dialog box for each — it depends upon the program. When the document is done printing (or when the document is sent to the PrintMonitor if you're using background printing), the document and program are automatically closed for you, and you're returned to the desktop.

Canceling the printing of a document

If you decide you want to cancel a print job while it is still printing from the program, you can press ⌘-period (that's the Command key along with a period) or the Esc key.

If you are using PrintMonitor and a document has been passed from the program to PrintMonitor, you need to open PrintMonitor (by choosing it from the Application menu) and then highlight the document you want to cancel. If you are canceling the document that is currently printing, highlight it and then click the Cancel Printing button. If you want to cancel one of the documents waiting to print, highlight it and then click the Remove From List button. The Cancel Printing and Remove From List button are in the same place, the name just changes depending upon what you select.

Scheduling when to print

To schedule a print job to print at a later time, you have to get background printing activated and you have to move quickly enough to get to PrintMonitor before the document actually prints. Once you're in PrintMonitor, select the document you want to schedule and click Set Print Time. A dialog box appears in which you can enter the date and time for the document to print, or you can select Postpone Indefinitely. After you click OK, you're returned to PrintMonitor where you can highlight the document to confirm its scheduled print time. If you want, you can close PrintMonitor and it will automatically open when it's time to print the document.

That second option, Postpone Indefinitely, is really misnamed because what it does is hold the document and prints the next time the printer is available. The following figure is an example of the dialog box you'll see when the printer becomes available.

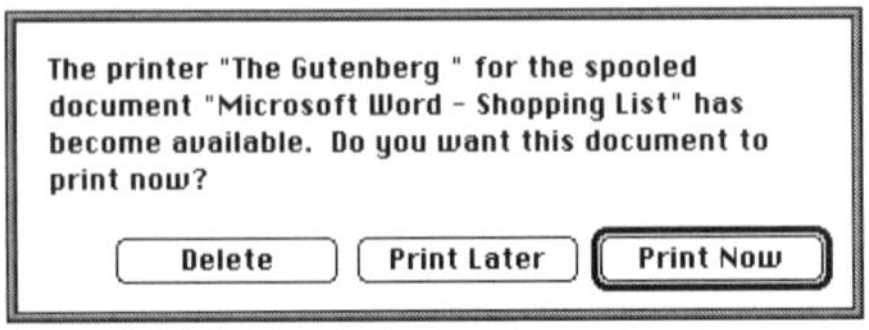

Changing the order of documents waiting to print

If you have a group of documents that are currently waiting to print, you can change their order by opening PrintMonitor and then dragging the documents into the order you want. Unfortunately, if you've scheduled a specific time for a document or if it's marked as Postpone Indefinitely, you can't change the order. When your printer isn't available, all of the documents you try to print are marked as Postpone Indefinitely, which means that you can't change their order.

Apple menu⇨Chooser

Use the Chooser to select and configure the current figure as well as connect to network servers.

Just the facts

Each printer you have installed on your system must have a printer driver in the Extensions folder within your System Folder. In addition, you may have printer drivers for printers you've never even heard of (System 7.5 installs the drivers for every Apple printer). Several printer drivers, plus the AppleShare control, are displayed in the following figure.

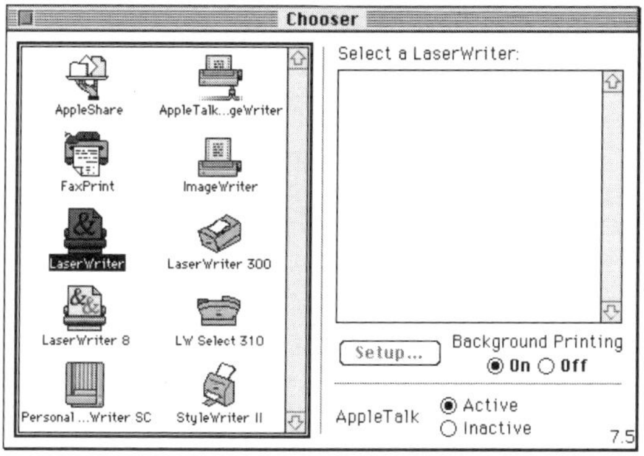

To select a printer, click the matching printer driver on the left of the window.

If the type of printer you select can be connected to your Mac in a number of ways, the box on the right contains the connection choices. If you're upgrading to System 7.5 and haven't changed how your printer is connected, you don't need to change any of these settings and can just close the window.

If the type of printer driver you select represents printers on a network, the box on the right contains a list of all of the printers of that type that are currently available throughout the network. Find the name of the printer you want to use and select it. If the printer you usually use is turned off, it won't appear in the list. If that's still the printer you want, don't select anything from the list. Your Mac remembers which printer you used and will continue to use that printer unless you tell it otherwise.

You can now close the Chooser window and start printing your document.

More stuff

In addition to just letting you select a printer, the Chooser now has a feature that enables you to update the printer files to more closely match the features available on your printer. To use this feature, select the printer you want and click the Setup button. As you move through the dialog boxes, Chooser updates its files to match the features that are actually available. If no Setup button is available, it means that your printer doesn't have any options that can be changed with this feature.

Using Apple menu⇨Chooser to work with a network is discussed in Part 8. Background printing is discussed under Application menu⇨PrintMonitor.

Application menu⇨PrintMonitor

Controls background printing, which enables you to continue working on your Mac while printing a document. Background printing is available for most printers, but you may decide it's not worth using if printing in the background causes your Mac to work so slowly that you can't really use it for anything else. Only while a document is actually printing is the PrintMonitor available on the Application menu (on the far right of the menu bar).

Just the facts

Very often, you'll use PrintMonitor without ever having to look at it. Each time you print a document using background printing, you activate PrintMonitor. Fortunately, the only time you need to use the command is when you want to check the status of the documents you have printing or when you want to have more control over their printing. When you open PrintMonitor, you see the PrintMonitor window, which looks just like the following figure.

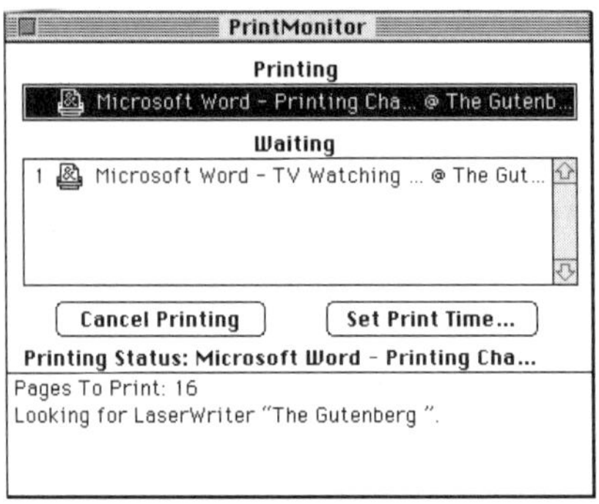

The PrintMonitor window shows the currently printing document, if any, in the top box and any documents waiting to print in the middle section. Canceling and scheduling documents is discussed in the first part of the chapter. Briefly, to stop a document from printing, click the button on the left (which will say either Cancel Printing or Remove From List). To schedule a document to print at a specific time, click the Set Print Time button. You get a dialog box where you can enter a date and time for the document to print. Finally, to change the order of the documents that are currently ready to print, simply highlight the document you want to reschedule and drag it to a new location on the list.

To stop printing entirely, choose File⇨Stop Printing (the last command on the File menu). When printing is stopped, the last command on the File menu becomes Resume Printing. Choose File⇨Resume Printing to begin printing the first document in the list.

You can also configure how PrintMonitor notifies you of problems and when you need to manually feed paper into your printer. To change these preferences, choose File⇨Preferences. Your choices include options for flashing the PrintMonitor as the icon for the Application menu, displaying an alert message in a dialog box, or both. You can also set your system so that it automatically displays the PrintMonitor window while printing, but that sort of defeats the purpose of background printing, which is to focus on other things (like a good game).

More stuff

When you select another program from the Application menu, the PrintMonitor window is automatically closed (unless you have changed PrintMonitor's preferences to always display the window).

When you install QuickDraw GX, the functions of PrintMonitor are replaced with the desktop printer and the Printing menu.

File⇨Page Setup

Sets the printer size and orientation as well as any special features available to you while printing (such as scaling the document or substituting fonts more appropriate for your printer). If you are working from within a program, you may find that the program adds its own options to the Page Setup dialog box as well. The options on the Page Setup dialog box work together with those you find on the Print dialog box.

Just the facts

After you choose File⇨Page Setup, you are faced with a dazzling array of options for telling your Mac what to expect from your printer. Of course, what features are available depend upon what printer you are using, but there are two that are common to most of the printers.

The first of the common choices is for the type of Paper. This option controls what size paper the program thinks you are using. Any margins that you set are measured from the edge of the paper.

The second of the common choices is for the Orientation of the paper. There are two choices — Portrait (the printing is across the narrowest edge of the paper) and Landscape (where the printing is across the longer edge of the paper). If you have an option for changing the orientation in Page Setup, it means that your printer can change which direction it prints — you don't have to move the paper.

More stuff

Previously, every page in a document had to have the same Page Setup options, but many newer programs allow you to set the options differently for sections of your document. For more information, check out the program's manual or, better yet, the appropriate *For Dummies* title.

TIP

Although they are not available for all printers, there are two additional settings which deserve special mention. The first, Precision Bitmap Alignment, is often hidden in a second dialog box that you get to by clicking on the Options button. Selecting Precision Bitmap Alignment causes most of your graphics to be printed slightly smaller (96% of their original size), but more clearly. The second setting, Font Substitution, is important because you need to know the danger it represents. When you select Font Substitution, you give your Mac permission to change any of the fonts in your documents to ones more suited to your printer. While this means that the print will appear crisper and clearer, it also means that what you get out of your printer won't match what's on your screen. It's much better to learn which fonts work well on your printer (experiment!) and avoid using any that give you poor results.

TIP

One of the first things you should do when you are creating a document that you intend to print is to make sure that you configure the settings in the Page Setup dialog box. This doesn't mean that you always have to keep opening the Page Setup dialog box. If you use the same Page Setup settings, you'll find that most programs remember the settings from the last time you printed. Some programs have a Default button on the Page Setup dialog box which you can click to store the current settings.

NOTE

Some "printer" choices, such as a fax modem, may change the name of the Page Setup command. For example, when I'm sending a fax, the command is File⇨Fax Setup.

File⇨Print

Actually prints your document and gives you some options that you may need to deal with, such as page range or number of copies. As with File⇨Page Setup, many programs add their own options to the Print dialog box.

Just the facts

You can choose File⇨Print from within a program or from the desktop. Either method gives you the same dialog box with its choices for the number of Copies and choices for which pages are to be printed. Once you've set all of the options the way you want them, click Print to get your document on paper.

There are usually a number of other choices on the Print dialog box which vary depending upon which printer you are using. You may be able to vary the quality of the printing, choose to print to a file (rather than the printer), or select a different paper source for various pages within the document. With System 7.5, many Print dialog boxes also have an Options button which you can click to see even more choices.

More stuff

NOTE

Some "printer" choices, such as a fax modem, may change the name of the Print command. For example, when I'm sending a fax, this command is File⇨Fax.

TIP

To use the Paper Source option (assuming it's available for your printer), you first need to have a document with more than one page. You can then click the First button to let your Mac know that the first page will be different from all the rest. You can then use the top list to pick the source for the first piece of paper and the lower list for the remaining pages.

Printing with QuickDraw GX

There are a lot of advantages to using QuickDraw GX and only one major disadvantage. The disadvantage is that it uses even more memory than System 7.5 by itself. With 8MB of working memory (RAM), you'll find that you barely have enough room to open a modern word processing package. Once the word processor is opened, you may find that you have to quit from the program before your documents will actually print. Of course, the solution is simple — get yourself about 24MB of RAM.

But QuickDraw GX does provide many new features. Some programs let you select your printer in the Print dialog box (rather than forcing you to open the Chooser). You have greater control over when and where your document prints and, if you are using a network, you can share a printer connected to your Mac with other users on the network (and remember, it's good to share).

With QuickDraw GX, you can install your printers as icons on your desktop. Every printer automatically has background printing (so that you can continue with other tasks while your document prints) and is controlled through a printing window. To display the printing window for a desktop printer, you simply double-click the printer's icon. (This printing window replaces many of the features of the old PrintMonitor.) The printing window shown here has several documents waiting to print.

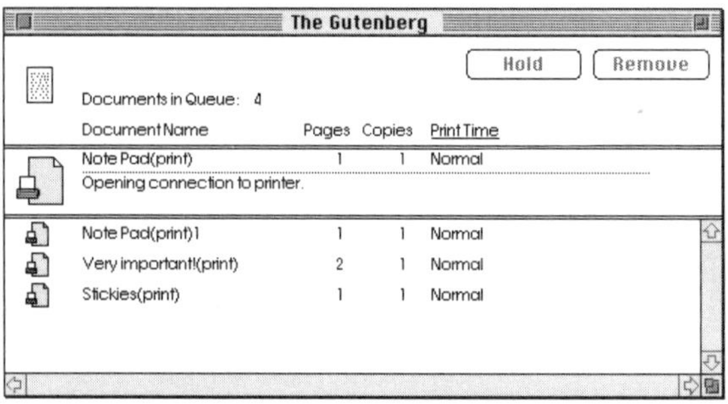

Finally, QuickDraw GX lets you create a Portable Digital Document (PDD), which can be read on any system that is running QuickDraw GX. It doesn't matter whether the other system has the program you used to create the document or the fonts that you used within the document. As long as the system is running QuickDraw GX, the PDD will look as good as it did on the system that created it.

If you want the benefits of QuickDraw GX but have programs that don't work well with the new technology, or if you want to be able to switch between using QuickDraw GX and the old-fashioned printing, you should install the QuickDraw GX Helper. Start the QuickDraw GX installation program and select Custom install. With the QuickDraw GX Helper on your system, you can select it from the Apple menu to turn QuickDraw GX on or off.

Installing a desktop printer

The first few steps for installing a printer are the same with or without QuickDraw GX. You have to make sure the printer is properly connected, and you have to find the proper printer driver and put it in the Extensions folder within your System Folder. In general, the name of the printer driver is the model name of your printer followed by the letters *GX*. If your printer is from Apple, the printer file is either on the System 7.5 disk you used to install your new system or, if your printer is newer than System 7.5, the printer driver may be on a disk that came with the printer. If you have some other type of printer, you may need to check with the manufacturer to get a GX-compatible printer driver. Here are the icons for the printers included with System 7.5.

Once you've got your printer drivers in the Extensions folder, choose Apple menu⇨Chooser. The new Chooser screen is shown in the following figure.

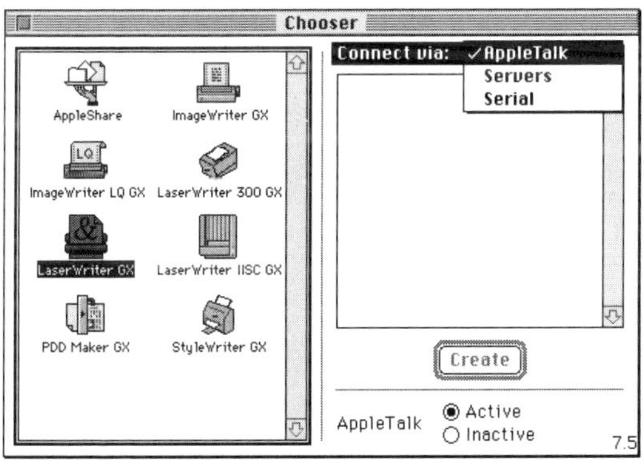

NEW 7.5

On the left of the window is a list of all of the GX printer drivers installed on your Mac. When you first open the Chooser, the right side of the window is blank. Find the driver that matches your printer and click it. The Connect via: pop-up menu appears in the upper-right corner of the window.

You need to use the choices on the Connect via: pop-up menu to connect to your printer. Of course, you need to know what the choices mean. *Server* means that the printer is actually connected to another computer that you connect to over your network. *Serial* means that the printer is plugged directly into your computer using either the modem or printer port. SCSI and AppleTalk are available for some printers and describe other ways that your printer might be connected to your Mac. In general, Server is the least likely choice, and, if it's available, AppleTalk is the most likely. If AppleTalk isn't an option, try Serial or SCSI (only one or the other will be available).

The window on the left now contains either a list of the available printers (by name) or, if you are using a serial connection, a choice between *Printer* and *Modem*. You need to pick the right choice to finish making the connection. Most printers that are connected with a serial connection are hooked to the printer port, so if you're not sure, try that choice first.

When you tell your Mac where to find your printer, the Create button (at the bottom right of the Chooser window) becomes available. Click it and your Mac installs a desktop printer using the information you have provided. Unfortunately, there isn't a message to tell you you're done, so you just have to try closing the window. When it closes, you'll find the icon for the desktop printer you just installed on the right side of your desktop. You can move it to a more convenient position, but don't try to put it into a folder. (Your Mac won't let you.)

NOTE

If you already had an Apple printer installed when you upgraded to QuickDraw GX, that printer is installed for you as a desktop printer. Isn't it great when you don't have to do anything?

REFERENCE

Another advantage of QuickDraw GX is that you can share a printer connected your Mac with other people over a network. For more information about networks, see Part 8. Creating portable documents with the PDD Maker printer file is discussed in the last section of this chapter.

Printing from the desktop

One of the nice things about the new QuickDraw GX printing technology is that all of the old ways still work. For example, you can highlight a file's icon and choose File⇨Print to print that file. Of course, it wouldn't be new technology if there weren't also new ways of doing things.

NEW 7.5

To print a document using the new method, just drag the icon for the file you want to print on top of the printer icon and release the mouse button. That's all there is to it. Rather than using PrintMonitor, you manage the document with the printer's printing window (which you get by double-clicking on the desktop printer icon).

Recognizing a desktop printer

OK, the basic desktop printer icon is really easy to recognize. It's on the desktop and looks like a little printer. What's important to know, however, is that the printer icon changes to let you know what's going on with the documents that you are printing. Most of the changes consist of adding a second symbol, such as a piece of paper or a warning triangle, to the standard printer icon. That same symbol appears in the printing window, which is where you control the documents that are printing. To display the printing window for a specific printer, double-click the printer's icon.

The other reason that it's important to be able to recognize the printer icons is that because sometimes you can't open the printing window. This is most commonly a problem when your computer doesn't have enough memory to continue printing while displaying the printing information. The icon can help you figure out what's going on.

This is the standard icon for a LaserWriter on the desktop. Of course, if your printer isn't a LaserWriter, the icon looks different, but you should get the idea. Some of the other possible icon styles are shown in the first topic in this section, "Installing a Desktop Printer."

What's the difference between the first and second icon you ask? Well, this icon represents a printer that is set as the default printer (the one your programs will try to use automatically). The only difference is that there is a heavy border around the icon.

This is the icon you see while your printer is printing a document. You're suppose to think of a little piece of paper moving through the printer. As soon as the document has been sent to the printer, the icon changes back to the standard icon.

This is a printer that's trying to get your attention. OK, it's really the standard icon plus the international symbol for a warning. To find out what's going on, double-click the printer icon. As soon as you fix the problem, the warning sign goes away and the printer should start working again.

See the little stop sign? It means that the printer has been stopped and won't start up again unless you open the printing window (by double-clicking the printer icon) and start it yourself. Usually, the only way a printer stops is if you told it to or if the printer is turned off.

This means that the printer you're trying to use doesn't exist any more. It could be that the printer's been unplugged or something's wrong with the connection. Most often, the easiest thing to do is recreate the desktop printer by installing it again with Apple menu➪Chooser. To get rid of the old desktop printer icon, drag it into the Trash.

Canceling the printing of a document

To cancel a print job, double-click the desktop printer to open the printing window. Find the job you want to cancel and click the Remove button (in the upper-right corner). That's all there is to it.

NOTE

With QuickDraw GX, a temporary QuickDraw document is created for each document you try to print. When you cancel the printing of a document, the temporary QuickDraw document is placed in the Trash. At some point, you need to empty the Trash to actually get rid of the temporary document. Don't worry, your original copy is fine. If you decide you really did mean to print the document, you can drag it from the Trash back into a printing window or onto a desktop printer. For some reason, when you drag it from the Trash, you'll get a copy instead of the original, but that's OK.

Scheduling when a document prints

NEW 7.5

With programs that are compatible with all of the System 7.5 printing features, the new QuickDraw GX technology lets you schedule your document to print at a specific time directly from the Print dialog box. Along the left side of the Print dialog box are a series of icons that represent the various printing options. Find the one that looks like a little clock face (with the Print Time label) and select it. If you don't see the icons along the left side, but you do have a button labeled More Choices, click the button and then check for the icon.

The Print Time options can be used to identify a document as Urgent (which moves it before any other documents with Normal priority), hold the document in the printer, set the document to print at a specific time, or give the document Normal priority (the standard setting). Simply select the scheduling option you want to use. If you are scheduling the document at a specific time, make any changes necessary to the date and time. Now, make any other decisions for the other printing options and then click the Print dialog box.

If your program doesn't provide you with all of these fancy options, you can still control the scheduling of your document — it's just more work. Print your document as normal and then quickly move back to the desktop (choose Finder from the Application menu on the far right). Double-click the desktop printer you are using to open its printing window. You can then select the document and use the options on the printing menu to schedule when the document will print. Use Printing⇨Hold Print Request to hold the document until you release it; use Printing⇨Set Print Time to assign a priority (either Urgent or Normal) or set a time for the document to print.

TIP

If you need to schedule a print time and the Print dialog box does not contain the Print Time option, you may want to go to the desktop printer and stop all printing before you send your document to the printer. Otherwise, by the time you move from your program to the printing window, your document may have already started printing. To stop all printing, use Printing⇨Stop Print Queue.

NOTE

If you put a document on hold, you need to use the Resume button or the Printing⇨Resume command to let your Mac know when you are ready for the document to print.

WARNING!

Be careful about assigning the Urgent priority to your documents, particularly if you work on a network with many other people. If everybody falls into the habit of assuming that their document should print first, and everybody starts assigning the Urgent priority to all of the documents, it no longer does any good. If everybody's documents are marked as Urgent, then the printing requests are handled on a first come, first served basis. And once this pattern starts, it's really hard to break. After all, who would want to print with Normal priority and have to wait hours before the document actually prints.

REFERENCE

The details of using the new Print dialog box are discussed under File⇨Print later in this section.

Changing the order of documents waiting to print

NEW 7.5

You need to open the printing window by double-clicking on the desktop printer. You can then drag the documents listed so that they represent the order you want them to print. The only restriction is that you cannot move a document with a Normal priority before one with an Urgent priority. See the previous topic, "Scheduling when a document prints," for information about changing a document's priority.

Previewing a document waiting to print

NEW 7.5

Although many programs offer a File⇨Print Preview command, there's now a way to check out a document after it's been sent to the printer. Double-click the desktop printer to open the printing window and then double-click the document you want to check. A QuickDraw GX version of the document is opened in SimpleText where you can move through the pages and check that what you're gonna get out of your printer is what you want.

Changing printers for a document

NEW 7.5

If you have more than one desktop printer on your Mac, you can move documents among them quite easily. You might want to do this if one printer is particularly slow or if you accidentally sent your document to the wrong printer to begin with. All you need to do is open the printing window where the document is (by double-clicking on the desktop printer) and drag the document from that printing window onto the desktop printer where you now want it to print. That's it. If you formatted the document specifically for the original printer, you may find that the document may not print as well on a different type of printer.

ATM GX

Controls the position and formatting of characters drawn with QuickDraw GX on your screen. Using Adobe Type Manager generally provides a closer match between what you see on the screen and what prints on the paper. In reality, the best way to decide what works for you is by experimenting with the various settings.

Just the facts

The ATM GX control panel is found in the Control Panels folder within your System Folder. You open this control panel by choosing Apple menu⇨Control Panels⇨ATM GX.

At the top of the control panel are a pair of buttons for turning the Type Manager on or off. Try printing a document containing several different fonts; then compare it to what you see on the screen both with and without the Type Manager turned on. If you don't see any improvement, and the documents prints in about the same amount of time, you can probably turn the Type Manager off.

On the left side of the control panel is a number box for setting the amount of memory used to store font information. Try increasing or decreasing this number to speed-up the display of fonts on-screen. ATM GX requires at least some memory to do its job, so there's a minimum value that you can't go below.

The most important controls are those on the right side which let you choose between preserving the *Line spacing* or the *Character shapes*. The reason you have to choose is that in many cases, your monitor can't match the printer's output exactly. When that happens, your Mac needs to know whether it is more important to place the letters where they will appear on the line or to maintain the shape they will have when printed. It's really a matter of personal choice. You need to decide which option is more important to you or, put another way, which one irritates you more.

ColorSync System Profiler

NEW 7.5

Provides the information needed by QuickDraw GX to change the colors used for a document on your screen. Using ColorSync ensures that if you move the document to another Mac with a different monitor, the colors will still look the same. It also helps to make sure that the colors on your screen match the ones you get from your printer (assuming you have a color printer).

Just the facts

All you really can do with this control panel is open it (via Apple menu⇨Control Panels⇨ColorSync System Profiler) and select your monitor. If your monitor isn't listed, you should select Set System Profile from the drop-down list and then go to the folder of profiles to find the proper information.

More stuff

NOTE

The actual profiles are kept in the ColorSync Profiles folder, which is in the Preferences folder within your System Folder.

File⇨Custom Page Setup

REFERENCE

Gives access to paper formats that do not appear in the normal File⇨Page Setup dialog box. This command only appears within programs that are compatible with System 7.5 and the QuickDraw GX technology. In general, the problem you may encounter is that some of the formats on the list may not actually work on your printer. For more information, see the entry for File⇨Page Setup.

File⇨Page Setup

NEW 7.5

Sets the paper type, orientation, and scaling for your document. In many programs, the same Page Setup dialog box is used for all printers if you are using QuickDraw GX.

Just the facts

Finally, there's a standard Page Setup dialog box available in most programs that doesn't change based on which printer you're using. Now, I don't know how much this actually helps most people who use Macs, but it makes life much simpler for those of us who write about using Macs. For one thing, I can now say that the following figure is the Page Setup dialog box you'll see when you have QuickDraw GX installed and choose File⇨Page Setup from the desktop (or any program that takes advantage of the new QuickDraw GX technology).

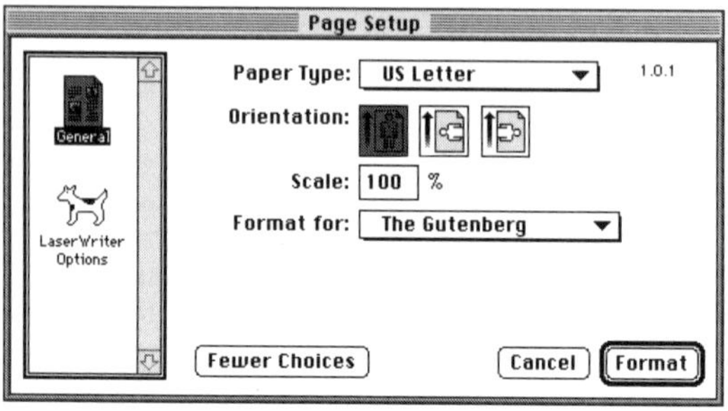

Other programs may have slightly different dialog boxes, but they are now much more consistent. In fact, even with the dialog box shown here, there are two versions — the smaller one you see if you click Fewer Choices and the larger one shown here.

NOTE

If you don't see all of the choices in the preceding figure, you can click the More Choices button in the lower left of the smaller dialog box you do see. Clicking that button expands the dialog box so that it looks like the one I've presented.

There are now three options that are common to almost all printers that appear on any version of the Page Setup dialog box. Paper Type controls what size paper the program thinks you are using. Any margins that you set are measured from the edge of the paper. Orientation has three choices — Portrait (printing is across the narrowest edge of the paper) and two versions of Landscape (printing is across the longer edge of the paper). Changing the Orientation in Page Setup changes the way your printer prints — you don't have to move the paper. The final choice, Scaling, lets you enlarge or reduce the document by a percent value. Two hundred percent is twice as large both horizontally and vertically, while 50 percent is half as large both horizontally and vertically. With the right utility (such as the Peirce Paper Saver included with System 7.5), you can use a 50-percent reduction and print four pages on a single sheet of paper

The Format for drop-down list lets you tell your Mac which printer you plan on using to print your document. Depending on the printer you select, you may be able to set additional options using the icons on the left of the dialog box.

File⇨Print

Used to actually print the document. Of course, there are still some last-minute options you can change, but when you finally get around to choosing File⇨Print, you're close to having a document in your hands.

Just the facts

As with the File⇨Page Setup dialog box, the Print dialog box is now more standardized. Unfortunately, there are still many programs (including Apple's own Note Pad) that don't take advantage of the new technology. In those that do, however, choosing FileÍPrint reveals the dialog box similar to the one shown here.

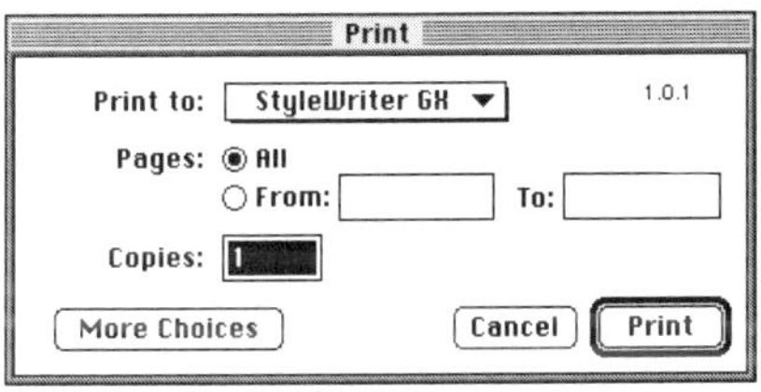

The most important feature is the Print to drop-down list at the top of the dialog box. You use this list to select which printer you are using for the document (no more going to the Chooser to change printers); it's all conveniently located on the Print dialog box. The other options are fairly easy to understand: you can select which pages you want to print and how many copies you want to print.

Down in the lower-right corner of the dialog box is a button labeled More Choices. Click that button to reveal the larger version of the dialog box shown in the following figure. (If you don't have a More Choices button, then either your program doesn't support all of the new features or you were already looking at the larger dialog box.)

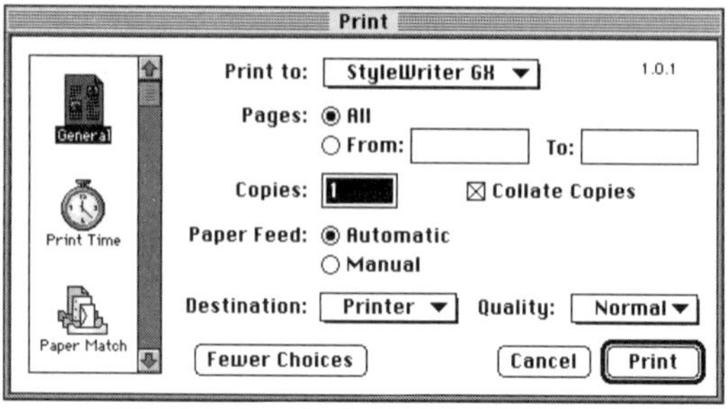

Notice that the icons along the left side represent various categories of options. Selecting one of the icons changes the remainder of the dialog box to show the various options in that category. For example, if you select Print Time, the dialog box changes to the one shown here.

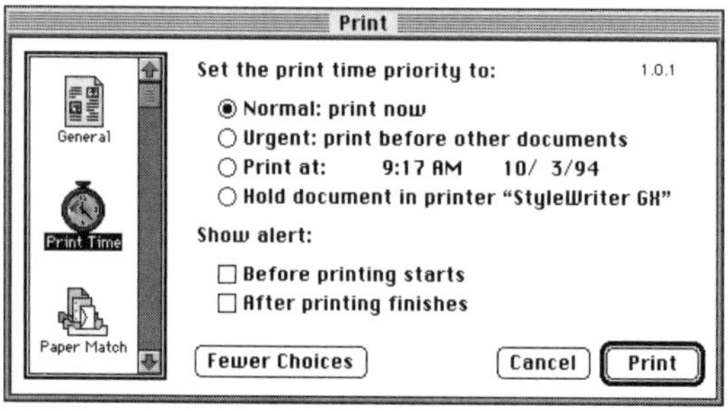

The standard categories are General (which has the options you are most likely to use frequently), Print Time (which is used to schedule when a document prints), and Paper Match (which is used with printers that can print with more than one type of paper from different trays). Depending on the printer you select, some options may have only one choice available. For example, with a LaserWriter, the only choice for Quality is Best. If you don't want to deal with having this many choices, click the Fewer Choices button to return to the simpler version of this dialog box.

More stuff

If a program doesn't use the dialog box shown in the "Just the facts" section, then the program doesn't fully support the new QuickDraw GX technology and will displal an old-fashioned Print dialog box for the current default printer. To change which desktop printer is the default, go to the desktop (by choosing Finder from the Application menu), click once on the printer you want to use, and then choose Printing➪Set Default Printer.

NOTE In addition to the General, Print Time, and Pape Match options, you may see additional options. Some of these are added by your program, and some of them represent printing extensions which have been installed for the desktop printer. To find out a bit more about printing extensions, see Printing➪Extensions Setup.

TIP The only standard option that really is worth its own tip is the Collate Copies check box. On many printers, selecting this option significantly slows down the printing of your copies. The reason is that many printers receive all of the information for a single page, and it's faster to make all of the copies of that page when it's first sent to the printer. That way, your Mac only has to send the information once. Otherwise, if you print the pages in order for each copy, each time your Mac prints a single copy of a page it has to send the information for that page all over again. If you need multiple copies of a multipage document, use a copier and save your printer from wear and tear.

WARNING! Even Apple admits that the QuickDraw GX technology is still in development. That means that parts of it don't work yet. One example is that there are a number of problems with using the Paper Match options, especially the Scale to Fit feature. All I can do is warn you about it because there isn't a solution yet. For now, you'll just have to wait until Apple fixes these problems.

REFERENCE I discuss the features in the Print Time category under the "Scheduling when a document prints" topic earlier in this section. Adding additional extensions is covered in PrintingÍExtensions Setup.

File➪Print One

REFERENCE Prints a single copy of the document using the default desktop printer and its standard settings. This means that you don't see a Print dialog box for the document and don't have a chance to change any of the settings. To find out more about the various options available and how to control them, see File➪Print. Note that the command's name may vary slightly. For example, in Microsoft Word, it becomes File➪Print One Copy.

Printing⇨Extension Setup

NEW 7.5

Selects which printing extensions are active and in what order they are displayed within the Print dialog box. Each extension is represented by it's own icon in the QuickDraw GX Print dialog box. Extensions are only available within programs that support QuickDraw GX.

Just the facts

Like other extensions, a printing extension must be placed in your Extensions folder within your Systems Folder in order to be available. Once the printing extension is in the Extensions folder, select the desktop printer which is to use the extension and then choose Printing⇨Extension Setup. All of the installed printing extensions are listed in the Extensions Setup dialog box. To make an extension available from the Print dialog box, put a check next to its name.

To change the order of the extensions icons in the Print dialog box, drag the extension names to the new order. The built-in General option is always displayed as the first icon; the built-in Print Time and Paper Match options are displayed as the last two icons.

Printing⇨Hold Print Request

NEW 7.5

Postpones printing the selected document(s) until you tell your Mac to resume printing. You can also select the document(s) and click on the Hold button to get the same effect. Other documents that are not on hold continue to print normally. No, your Mac doesn't play elevator music when you put a document on hold. To stop all the documents from printing, use Printing⇨Stop Print Queue.

Printing⇨Input Trays

NEW 7.5

Informs your Mac what type of paper is in each of your printer's trays. You need to provide this information before you can use the Paper Matching option in the Print dialog box. The Input Trays Setup dialog box contains a list of paper types for each of your input trays. Many printers only have one tray, so you may only have one choice.

Printing➪Resume on Page . . .

Starts printing the selected document on a specific page. You use this command to restart a document that stopped printing because of a printer problem or to start a document that you placed on hold using Printing➪Hold Print Request (or the Hold button). The number you enter in the Resume Print Request dialog box is the number of the physical page, which may be different from the page number if you are printing a title page or if your document is organized in sections. Clicking the Resume button is the same as choosing this command.

Printing➪Resume on Page One

Starts printing a document that is on hold or that failed to print completely. As you might imagine, the entire document is printed starting with page one. To resume printing on a specific page, which you often want to do if part of a document printed before the problem occurred, you need to use Printing➪Resume On Page.

Printing➪Set Default Printer

Makes the current desktop printer the default printer, which is the one that will be used by programs that don't support the selection of different printer from the Print dialog box. You can have only one default printer selected at a time. The icon for the default printer is indicated with a heavy black border.

Printing➪Set Print Time

Schedules the selected document(s) for printing. You can either move a document to the start of the list by assigning an Urgent priority or enter a date and time for the document to print. The third choice on the dialog box, Normal, is what documents usually have and basically tells your Mac to print the document when it's convenient.

Printing⇨Start Print Queue

NEW 7.5

Tells your Mac that the printer is ready to work. You use this command if you stopped the printing for some reason (using Printing⇨Stop Print Queue) or if a printing problem occurred that caused your Mac to assume the printer wouldn't be available. As soon as you choose the Printing⇨Start Print Queue command, the first document in the list should start preparing to print.

Printing⇨Stop Print Queue

NEW 7.5

Prevents any documents from printing. The current document, if any, stops printing and is put at the top of the list of waiting documents. You use this command when you need to make changes to the printer or when there is some sort of printing problem.

View⇨By Copies

NEW 7.5

Changes the order of the list of documents in the printing window so that the ones with the most copies requested are at the start of the list. You can click any of the column names (Copies, Pages, and so on) to change the order of the list.

View⇨By Document Name

NEW 7.5

Arranges the documents in the printing windows so that they are in alphabetical order by document name (from A to Z). To change to another organization, click a column name (Copies, Pages, and so on) to sort by that column.

View⇨By Pages

NEW 7.5

Sorts the list of documents in the printing window so that those with the highest number of pages are at the start of the list. To sort by the information in a different column, click the column name (Copies, Pages, and so on).

View⇨By Print Time

NEW 7.5

Puts the documents in the printing window in the order that they will print. This is the normal view for a printing window. To use the information in another column to organize the documents, click the column name (Copies, Pages, and so on).

Portable Digital Documents

NEW 7.5

A Portable Digital Document (PDD) is one that contains all the information it needs to display or print itself on any Macintosh system. Imagine that you have spent hours working on a document and have a single copy on your disk. Just before your big presentation, you realize that you've misplaced your printed copy. Even if you're lucky enough to find a Macintosh with the right software, it might not have the same fonts. Without the right fonts, the text of the document may become unreadable, and it's likely that the layout of the document will change in unpleasant ways.

Sample PDD

These kinds of problems may disappear with the introduction of QuickDraw GX and PDDs. Any document can be printed to the PDD Maker GX and converted into a PDD. You don't need to change anything about the programs you use; you just select the PDD Maker GX as your printer. PDDs have their own icons (shown in the figure to the left) and can be viewed and printed on any system with QuickDraw GX.

Before QuickDraw GX, if you tried to work with a document when you didn't have the original fonts it used, the odds were good that the results would be less than perfect and often hard to read. In fact, in some cases, the results weren't readable at all. Some programs try to substitute other fonts, but the line spacing and formatting usually change. Even worse is the situation in which someone gives you a file, and you don't have the program used to create the document. In that case, you may not be able to even open the document. With PDDs, the fonts are stored as part of the document itself, so they're available whenever you open the document. Furthermore, PDDs are designed so that they can be opened without a specific application. You can print them and even view them on your screen without having to worry about what program was used to create the document.

There is, of course, a downside. Because the font information is stored as part of PDDs, the documents can get quite large. Fortunately, most well-designed documents only use a few fonts, so while small files get much larger, larger files only grow a little bit.

Making a Portable Digital Document

You have to first create a desktop PDD Maker by selecting the PDD Maker GX extension in the Chooser and then clicking the Create button. Of course, to use PDDs, you must have installed QuickDraw GX on your Mac.

If your program fully supports QuickDraw GX, you create a PDD by choosing File⇨Print and then selecting PDD Maker GX from the Print to list. Because you're creating a file rather than a document, you have to provide a file name for the new document. You can check the Auto-name PDD Files box to have your Mac use the original document's file name with *PDD* appended to it. You can also leave that box blank and provide a name in the dialog box that appears when you click Save.

If your program doesn't fully support QuickDraw GX, you can still create PDDs. Simply make the PDD Maker GX your default printer (by clicking it once and choosing Printing⇨Set Default Printer). The dialog box you get when you choose File⇨Print will have a Save button, and when you click Save, you'll get a dialog box for naming the file. The second dialog box (where you provide the file name) is also where you decide which fonts to include with the PDD.

There's only one special item you need to pay attention to when creating a PDD. Instead of choices about the quality of the output, the PDD Maker GX dialog box has a list for selecting which fonts to include. The more fonts you include, the more portable your document. Unfortunately, they also make your document bigger. If you select No Fonts, the person trying to open the document will be able to see its contents but may not be able to actually read the text. That person's Mac will have to substitute the closest fonts it has. If you decide to use the All Fonts option, your document can be opened on any system and the output will look the same as it did on your own. The middle ground is to select Non-standard fonts, which creates a document that will probably display clearly because other systems are likely to have the required fonts.

Part 8

Playing Post Office with PowerTalk

Probably the most difficult things to learn when working with a Mac on a network are all the special words used to describe things. Certainly working with a Mac on a network is easier than any other computer's solution, but talking about networking isn't. One of the things that makes a Mac network so much easier to use is that most of the equipment you need is already built into your Mac; the only things you need are the right cables to connect the network.

All of the most important terms sound the same—*AppleTalk*, *AppleShare, LocalTalk, EtherNet, EtherTalk, PowerTalk* and *PowerShare*. AppleTalk refers to the methods used by your Mac and the equipment on the network to communicate. You can think of AppleTalk as the language used by Apple equipment to talk to each other. *AppleShare* is a collection of features that uses the AppleTalk language to let you share files and folders with other computers.

Originally, AppleTalk was designed to work on a specific type of cable, called LocalTalk, but new Macs have technology built in that lets them use EtherNet cabling. Both LocalTalk and EtherNet refer to specific types of cabling that is plugged into the equipment to create the physical network. EtherNet is much faster than LocalTalk, and in order for your Mac to keep up, you need to have EtherTalk, which adds some new vocabulary to the AppleTalk language.

PowerTalk is the newest upgrade to the Mac network language and contains a variety of tools to expand what sort of things can be done across the network. PowerShare refers to the technology that takes advantage of these new parts of the network's language. To summarize, Macs started out running AppleTalk over LocalTalk cabling, but now the most advanced Mac networks now run AppleTalk with the EtherTalk and PowerTalk additions over EtherNet cabling.

In addition to expanding the network's language, System 7.5 contains a number of built-in commands to take advantage of these new tools. The *Mail* commands enable you to send messages between users on the network; *Key Chains* makes it much easier to connect and reconnect to a group of locations and services on the network; *Catalogs* provide a tool for organizing the information you need to effectively use your network and your mail program.

To connect to other computers to use their files (that is, to connect to *servers*) or to connect to a printer over the network, all you need are the proper extensions for your network and the Chooser. To let others use files on your computer, you need to use a special pair of control panels—Sharing Setup and Users &

Groups — as well as the File➪Sharing command. To share a printer connected to your computer, you need those two control panels plus File➪Get Info. You also use the File Sharing Monitor control panel to keep track of who is using your computer. To choose the type of network connection and to check out the version of the network technology you are using (such as what version of AppleTalk, EtherTalk, and LocalTalk), you use the Network control panel. Finally, to turn on or off the new features of PowerTalk, you need to use the PowerTalk Setup control panel.

The mail features are controlled by the commands that appear on the Mailbox menu. To get to the Mailbox menu, you need to have a mailbox (like the one shown in the figure to the left) on your desktop. To send a mail message, your program must have a File➪Mail or similar command. (System 7.5 includes the AppleMail program, which can be used to send messages if none of your other programs are appropriate.) Although you can change the name of the mailbox on your own desktop (which changes the name that is put on messages you send), to change the name that other people see when sending you a message, you must use the Sharing Setup control panel.

Double-clicking the mailbox opens your mail trays and lets you work with the various mail messages as well as set preferences. When you get a mail message, how you're notified is controlled by the Mailbox➪Preferences command. The View menu is used to organize the list of messages in your mail tray. Because one of the greatest concerns about electronic mail is its security, Apple includes the DigiSign Utility, which creates electronic signatures used to verify that no changes are made to a document after you sign it.

The catalog feature is used to create lists of people, network places, or services that you can then use to streamline your work on the network. The services available through your Key Chain are stored in the Catalogs catalog, which appears on your desktop when PowerTalk is active. Like all catalogs, it looks like a book, but you can identify the Catalogs catalog by the world map displayed across its pages. The Catalogs catalog contains catalogs for each of the types of services available to you on the network. For example, the AppleTalk catalog lists all of the AppleTalk connections that you have used.

You can also create personal catalogs (identified by a face on one of the pages) to keep track of information about the people you communicate with. The contents of catalogs are controlled by the commands on the Catalog menu, and the listings within the catalogs are controlled by the View menu.

?⇨PowerTalk Guide

Reveals all of Apple's wisdom concerning the PowerTalk features. You only see this command if you've installed PowerTalk along with System 7.5.

Just the facts

To get to the information about PowerTalk, simply select ?⇨PowerTalk Guide. As with most Apple guides, you have a choice of looking for a specific keyword or combination of keywords, searching through the alphabetical index, or viewing a list of the main topics covered. To get a better understanding of what PowerTalk actually provides for you, I suggest starting with the Topics list.

More stuff

REFERENCE

For general information on using the new Apple Guide technology, see ?⇨Macintosh Guide in Part 2.

Apple menu⇨Chooser

Provides access to any available AppleShare services. In other words, the Chooser enables you to hook-up to other Macintoshes on your network to share files (in addition to all of the functions the Chooser provides that are associated with printing).

Just the facts

When you choose Apple menu⇨Chooser, the Chooser window appears with all of your installed printing and network extensions shown in the left half. To use the Chooser to hook-up to other resources on the network, you need to first click the AppleShare icon in the upper-left corner. With the AppleShare icon selected, the right side of the Chooser shows a list of all the Macs on your network that are willing to share their files (each of these Macs is a *file server*). When you find the Mac that has the files you wish to use, double-click its name to open a connection to that Mac. After you double-click the Mac you want to use, you are asked to identify yourself and provide a password using the dialog box shown here.

Enter the name of your account on the other Mac in the Name text box and your password in the Password box. If you don't have an account, you can try connecting as a guest by clicking the Guest button. If your account doesn't have a password, leave the

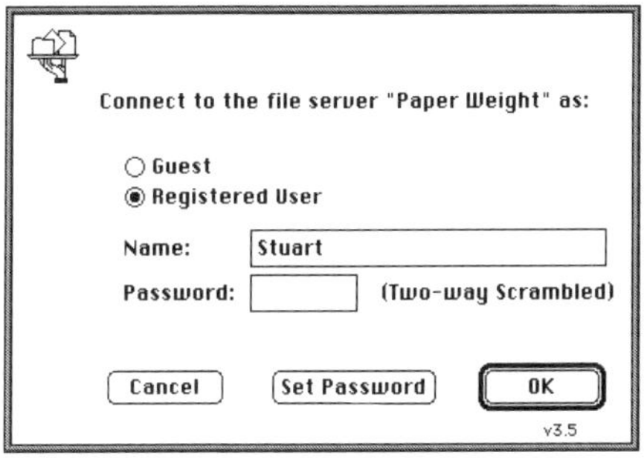

Password box blank. After you enter the information, click the OK button. You then get a dialog box where you can select the folders or disks you wish to use. This dialog lists all of the folders and disks available on the other computer. Items for which you have permission to access appear normally in the list. Items for which you don't have permission to access are grayed out in the list.

To select one of the items from the list, click it once. On the right side of the list, next to each name, is a check box. If you put a check next to an item, every time you start your Mac, it will try to reestablish the connection to that item. After you have selected all of the items that you wish to open, click the OK button.

Without PowerTalk, if you put a check next to any of the names, you will be asked whether you want to save your password for reestablishing the connection. The advantage to saving your password is that your Mac will be able to reconnect as long as the item is available. The disadvantage is that anybody turning on your computer will have access to the files on that server. If the purpose of using passwords is to provide any measure of security for the files, you should not save your password. With PowerTalk, you are asked if you want to add the connection to your Key Chain. If you add the connection to your Key Chain, you will only need to provide your Key Chain Access Code (password) to open the connection.

Each of the items you connect to appear on your desktop with the AppleShare icon. You can use these items the same way you use a disk inserted in your machine. The owner of the server to which you are connected determines your access privileges to the files and folders with the File⇨Sharing command on his or her Mac.

More stuff

NOTE

On larger networks, you may have a choice of which zone you are using. A zone is a grouping of Macs on the network. If your network has zones, you'll need to select the zone first to see a list of the Macs in that zone.

TIP

When you are connecting to a file server, you can use ⌘-G to select connecting as guest and ⌘-R to select connecting as a registered user.

NOTE

You can use the Set Password button to change your password on the other Macintosh.

TIP

To break a connection to another computer, drag the AppleShare icon for that connection into the Trash. To stop automatically reconnecting to a service when you start your Mac, you need to break the connection and then go through the process of reconnection manually. This time, when you get to the dialog box where you create the connection, remove the check next to the name. After removing the check, create the connection. You have to go through all of these steps to let your Mac know that you no longer want to connect at startup.

NOTE

If both your Mac and the one you connect to are using QuickDraw GX, you may also be able to use printers that are connected directly to the other computers.

REFERENCE

To connect to another Mac, you have to have an account on that Mac (created on that system using the Users & Groups control panel) and file sharing on that Mac has to be turned on (using the Sharing Setup control panel). With PowerTalk, Apple menu⇨Key Chain provides a more secure way of storing your connections to other computers.

Apple menu⇨Key Chain

Stores information about any resources that you use across the network in your Catalogs catalog (on your desktop). The advantage to setting up a Key Chain is that it provides a central record of all of the services that you use and lets you get to them with a single password.

Just the facts

Choose Apple menu⇨Key Chain (or Apple menu⇨Mail and Catalogs⇨Key Chain or Catalogs⇨Configure Catalogs) to add or remove services. When you click the Add button, your Mac lists all of the available types of services. Select the service or services you want to add and click the OK button. Your Mac then displays a list of all of the PowerTalk network services that it can locate in those categories. To remove a service, select the service and click the Remove button.

To change the password used for your Key Chain (called the *Access Code*), click the Change Code button. You need to know your old password (obviously) and to have a new password ready to enter. Enter both the old and new passwords and click OK. You are then told that you need to enter the new password a second time. Fine, you should always do what your Macintosh tells you, so after you get rid of the message, go ahead and type the new password again and click OK.

I don't know why this command appears in so many places. I think it must be that it's the heart of the new PowerTalk and they wanted to be sure you noticed it.

More stuff

Use the PowerTalk Setup to control when the Key Chain is automatically locked and the Special⇨Lock Key Chain and Special⇨Unlock Key Chain to manually control whether the Key Chain is locked.

Apple menu⇨Mail and Catalogs

Mail and Catalogs is actually a folder in the Apple Menu Items folder within your System Folder. It contains aliases to many of the more common commands that you may want to use with your mailbox and catalogs. In addition, it's probably the best place to store any catalogs that you create for your own use.

You may find that your Mac put your Key Chain command in this folder rather than directly onto the Apple menu. For more information, see Apple menu⇨Key Chain. Creating new catalogs and working with the ones you've got are discussed under Catalogs⇨New Personal Catalog. The Find in Catalog utility is discussed in a tip under the same topic. Finally, the AppleMail program has its own entry following this one.

AppleMail

The AppleMail program is included with System 7.5 but has its own menus and features. Although most word processors and many other types of applications have the File⇨Mail command to let you send their documents as mail messages, there are advantages to using a specialized program like AppleMail.

Just the facts

You start AppleMail the same way you start any program; however, the odds are good that its already been installed on your Apple menu as Apple menu⇨Mail and Catalogs⇨AppleMail. The most important part of the AppleMail screen is the Mailer at the top of the document. In the following figure the Mailer is shown above the newspaper headline.

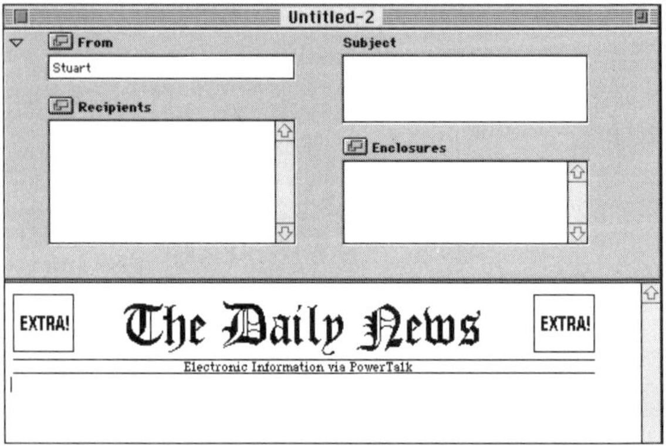

There are four sections to the Mailer, three of which must be completed before you send your document. The Sender is automatically filled in as the current Key Chain owner. To change the Sender you can click the button next to the word *From* to open a dialog box that lets you change Key Chains or PowerShare accounts. When you click the button next to the word *Recipients,* you see the dialog box shown here.

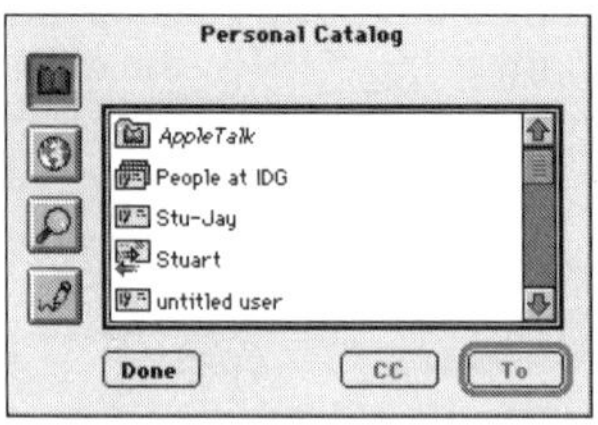

The four buttons on the left side of the dialog box are used to select the source for the recipients' names. The top button lists the contents of your preferred personal catalog (set using File⇨Get Info). The second icon, with a globe on it, is used to browse the contents of other catalogs on the network. You can select an individual's address, an individual information card, or a group from any of the catalogs. The third button, with the magnifying glass, lets you search for a specific name. The fourth button allows you to write in an address without having to locate it on the network. You can include as many recipients as you want. To have the individual or group listed as a recipient, select the name and click the To button. After you enter all the names you want (including any carbon copies as described in the "More stuff" section), click the Done button.

In addition to at least one name for Recipients, you must also provide a subject. Simply click in the Subject box and type the heading for your mail message.

If you wish to send a file or group of files with your message, use the button next to Enclosures. Clicking the Enclosures button opens a dialog box where you can select files to be enclosed with your mail message. A file that is enclosed with a message is sent in its original format and can be used by the recipient.

At the top of the Mailer in the left corner (just below the window's close box) is a little triangle. Click that triangle to expand or collapse the view of the Mailer. When the Mailer is collapsed, it shows only the name of the sender and the first line of the subject information.

The Font, Size, Style, and most of the Edit menu work exactly like their counterparts in any Mac word processing program. In addition to these menus for working with text, the Edit menu also contains commands for recording and playing sounds.

The File menu contains the standard Macintosh File commands, as well as a command for Letterheads. Use the File⇨Letterheads command to open a new document using one of the Letterhead formats stored in the AppleMail Letterheads folder within the Preferences folder. Notice that you can design your own document and save it as a Letterhead by using the File⇨Save As Letterhead command.

The Mail menu contains commands both for sending a letter and reading a message. Mail⇨Send opens a dialog box that lets you assign a format for the message as well as a priority. If you want the recipient to be able to use the AppleMail program to read and respond to the message, you should send it with an AppleMail format. When you are reading a message, the Mail Reply and Mail Forward commands will be available. Mail Forward attaches a new Mailer (on top of the old one) where you can add your own Recipients as well as change the subject and add additional enclosures. Mail Reply opens a dialog box where you can select a Letterhead format for your reply (or use a blank format) and select between sending the response to all of the recipients plus the sender, or to the sender only.

The final commands on the Mail menu are useful for managing your mailbox. You can use Mail⇨Tag to assign a tag to any letter you have received. When working with your mailbox, you can choose to view the list of letters organized by tag. Mail⇨Open Next Letter opens the next letter waiting in the In Tray of your mailbox.

More stuff

TIP In addition to including someone as a Recipient, you can also send a copy of the letter as a carbon copy (by clicking the CC button). Normally, everyone who gets a copy of the message is listed as a recipient with those who were sent a carbon either marked with CC or listed as a separate group. In some programs, however, you can also send a blind carbon copy (usually by clicking a BCC button). A blind carbon copy is sent without including the recipient's name on any of the other copies.

NOTE Many programs include a File⇨Mail command, which enables you to add a Mailer to a document created in the program and often gives you access to the commands found on the Mail menu within AppleMail. Of course, developers can change how they decide to organize the commands and dialog boxes for sending mail, but the information present here should serve as a good, general overview.

TIP The way your name appears in other people's Recipients list is determined by the entry for the Macintosh name in the Sharing Setup control panel on your Mac. When you send a message, the name used for the From information is taken from your Key Chain (which is also the name of your mailbox). In other words, the name you use when you send mail and the name other people use when they send mail to you may be entirely different. Fortunately, you can always use the Reply feature to respond to a message that someone else has sent you — even if you don't know the right name to use.

REFERENCE The commands for managing documents in your mailbox are found on the Mailbox menu. For information about creating a personal catalog that contains information about people you might want to mail to, see Catalogs⇨New Personal Catalog.

Catalogs⇨Configure Catalogs

REFERENCE Catalogs⇨Configure Catalogs is just another incarnation of Apple menu⇨Key Chain. You can use this command to add new catalogs of services and update your existing catalogs. For more information about functions, see Apple menu⇨Key Chain.

Catalogs⇨New Group

Adds a group to the current personal catalog. A group is used with a mail program to enable you to send a message to all of the people in the group without having to enter each of the group members' names.

Just the facts

To create a group, you must first be in the catalog that will contain the group. Then choose the Catalogs⇨New Group command and, after the entry for the group appears in the catalog window, type the name for the group. You can fill your group by dragging existing entries onto the group icon. If the name is in the same catalog, dragging it will move it to the group. If you want to leave the name where it was and add a copy, hold down the Option key while dragging the name. If you drag a name from another catalog, it is always copied.

More stuff

TIP: To get rid of a group, drag it to the Trash. You can also move groups between catalogs by dragging them from one catalog window to another (or onto another catalog icon). To copy a group, hold down the Option key while dragging.

REFERENCE: Use Catalogs⇨New User to create entries for people in your catalog. Use Catalogs⇨New Personal Catalog to create a new catalog and File⇨Get Info to set the preferred catalog (which makes that catalog the one that will display automatically in most mail programs). For more information about organizing catalogs, see Catalogs⇨New Personal Catalog.

Catalogs⇨New Personal Catalog

Creates a new catalog which can then be filled with electronic addresses, information cards for individual users, group entries, and even aliases of other catalogs. A group entry contains aliases of one or more user entries and is used in a mail program to send the same message to everyone within the group.

Just the facts

Personal catalogs are the electronic address books you use to communicate with others over your network or via commercial networks (such as Internet). You can create as many catalogs as you wish, but it is important to make sure that the information they contain is organized. One, and only one, of your catalogs is identified as your preferred catalog (with the File⇨Get Info command). The information in your preferred catalog is available in most mail programs by clicking the Personal Catalog button (with its book icon) in the Recipients dialog box. Other catalogs are available within most mail programs by using the Catalog Browser button (with its globe icon).

Information that is for your own use should go into your preferred catalog. Putting it here makes it a bit easier to get to when you need to send a mail message. In general, you want to create a separate catalog only if you intend to share the information in it with others on the network. Other people will be able to use the Catalog Browser to view the information in the catalog and use it in their own mail programs.

Create a new catalog by choosing Catalogs⇨New Personal Catalog. If you are in a folder, the catalog is created within that folder. If you are viewing another catalog, the new catalog is created on the desktop. You now need to type a name for the catalog and make sure it's in the right location. Unless you have reason not to, I suggest storing all of your personal catalogs in the Mail and Catalogs folder within the Apple Menu Items folder.

After creating a new personal catalog, you need to put things into it. You can put an alias of another catalog into your new personal catalog by dragging the other catalog's icon onto your new personal catalog. You can create an information card for an individual by using Catalogs⇨New User. You can create a new group of individuals by choosing Catalogs⇨New Group and then dragging the individual's entries onto the group.

More stuff

TIP

Apple menu⇨Mail and Catalogs⇨Find in Catalog activates the Find in Catalog program, which can be used to locate an individual or group in any of the available catalogs. You have to know the starting character for the item you are seeking. This is similar to the tool that you can use within the Recipients dialog box in most mail programs to find an address. You can look for information cards for individuals (Users), for File Servers (a Catalogs catalog), or for other types of information. You can also restrict the search to specific locations. After you've found items that match your request, you can select the items you may want to use later and click the Save button to add an alias for each to your preferred catalog.

NOTE

You can add catalogs from your Catalogs catalog (the one with the world spread across its pages on the desktop) to any personal catalog. Doing so makes it easier to find an electronic address or other network information.

To find out about adding electronic addresses and individual information cards to your catalog, see Catalogs⇨New User. For information about making a catalog your preferred catalog, see File⇨Get Info.

Catalogs⇨New User

Creates an information card for an individual. These cards are stored within your catalogs and can be organized into groups of users. Although their primary purpose is to record electronic addresses, you can also use the information card to store other facts about a person as well.

Just the facts

You must be within a catalog to create an information card. Choose Catalogs⇨New User and then type the name for the information (generally some version of the person's name). Then, to fill in the information about the individual, double-click the user's entry. The Business Card view of the information card is shown in the following figure.

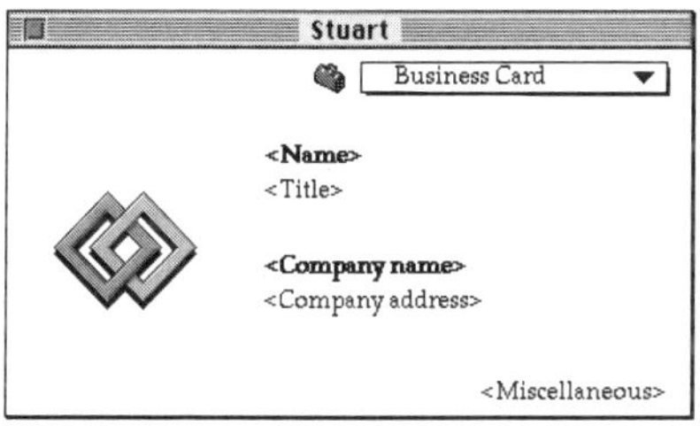

You can replace any of the text with the proper information as well as add your own image in place of the graphic shown in the figure. To change the placeholder text to the actual information, click the text and start typing. The placeholder will be replaced with whatever you type. For a cleaner look, if you aren't going to use one of the sections, highlight the placeholder text and press delete to remove it.

Each information card contains four views — Business Card, Personal Info, Phone Numbers, and Electronic Addresses. In order to use the information card with your mail system, you must include at least one entry in the Electronic Addresses view.

To add an electronic address, first gather the information you would enter to send a message to the individual electronically. This information should include the type of connection, the name of the computer account, and its location. Click the Add button and select the type of connection. The entry is created in the Electronic Addresses view. A dialog box then opens where you can enter the account name and location. After you complete the information in the dialog box, close it and then type a name for the address. Generally, the address's name should indicate the kind of system used to send the message. For example, you might have names like *Stuart's Internet Address* or *SjS on AppleTalk*.

More stuff

TIP If you want to record the address of someone who has sent you a message, you can drag the address from the mail message onto the desktop and from there onto the Electronic Addresses view of the information card. This method is much easier than trying to find a piece of scratch paper to write the address down and then typing it in later. If you can view a mail message and a blank information card at the same time, you can drag the address directly to the card. If you drag the information directly to the catalog window, you create an electronic address (without an entire information card).

REFERENCE For information on organizing your catalogs, see Catalogs⇨New Personal Catalog.

DigiSign Utility

Provides a method to verify that no changes have been made in the document after it was sent. You can use this new PowerTalk technology with any type of document, not just mail messages.

Just the facts

To check a mail message, click the Signer button at the bottom of the mailer. To check a document on the desktop, choose File⇨Get Info and click the Signer button. The Signer button (shown here at left) appears to the right of the comments box. The resulting dialog box lets you know if the file has been changed or if it is verified.

To place a verifying signature on your own documents, you need to obtain an actual signer file with your electronic signature. To get your signature, open the DigiSign Utility (in the PowerTalk folder within Apple Extras) and choose File⇨New Request. Complete the information in the dialog box and then save the request. You need to print out the request and mail it to the address on the bottom of the form. You'll get back a disk with the approval information which you can use to verify your own signature and create the signer file.

To use your signature, you can either drag a document onto the signer file or, in many mail programs, check the Sign Document option.

More stuff

TIP

The Apple Extras folder includes an approved signer called Demonstration Signer, which you are supposed to be able to use to see how the DigiSign features work. Unfortunately, it seems that Apple forgot to tell you where to get the identification code you need to use the signer. However, since they included the signer for you to practice with, I think they meant for you to be able to use it. The secret, hidden identification code you need is, what else, the word *password*. Of course, since everybody who has System 7.5 has this demonstration signer, using the demonstration signer doesn't provide any security. You can play around with it and send messages to yourself to see how the system works.

File Sharing Monitor

Selecting the File Sharing Monitor control panel displays a dialog box that lists all of the people who are currently using resources on your Mac and which items they are using. You can highlight a user's name and click the Disconnect button if you no longer want that person connected to your Mac. Don't ever disconnect a user as a joke — the odds are good that the person will lose whatever he or she is working on.

File⇨Get Info

There are a number of features that are added to the Get Info dialog box when you are using PowerTalk. Among these are a button for checking for changes to a document that has been verified with DigiSign signatures; a text box displaying the tags for your mail documents; a button for locating or setting the preferred catalog; and a box for entering the location of a QuickDraw GX printer.

Just the facts

What you see when you choose File⇨Get Info depends upon what type of icon you have selected. Some of the dialog box are just very terse descriptions, such as this one for the Catalogs catalog on your desktop, shown here.

Others, such as the one shown in the following figure for a QuickDraw GX printer, have text boxes where you can add information that can be used by others on the network. With printers, you may want to include a location so that others know where to come and look for their output.

Although not shown here, you can use File⇨Get Info to set the limits on the number of entries stored in your mailbox. Click once on your mailbox and then choose File⇨Get Info. There is a text box at the bottom of the dialog box where you can enter the maximum number of letters to be stored.

When you select a personal catalog and then choose File⇨Get Info, the dialog box has two additional buttons. The one on the left, Set Preferred, makes the selected catalog the preferred catalog. The preferred catalog can be identified by the red ribbon that appears on the left page of the icon and by the fact that it is the one used by most mail programs. The other button, Find Preferred, opens the folder containing the preferred catalog and highlights the catalog's icon.

More stuff

The standard parts of the Get Info window are discussed as part of File⇨Get Info in Part 2. The DigiSign signature is discussed under the entry for the DigiSign Utility earlier in this part.

File⇨Mail

This command appears in many programs and is, in fact, a menu of its own with all of the commands necessary for sending mail messages. These commands are discussed under the entry for AppleMail earlier in this part.

File⇨Sharing

Grants or restricts permission to the current folder or printers for other users. Permissions may be granted to guests (anyone who's made a connection), specific users, or groups of users. You can also change who owns a folder; the owner is the only person who can change the permissions for the folder.

Just the facts

To start, select the folder or printer that you intend to share and choose File⇨Sharing. If you select a folder, you should see a dialog box resembling the one shown here.

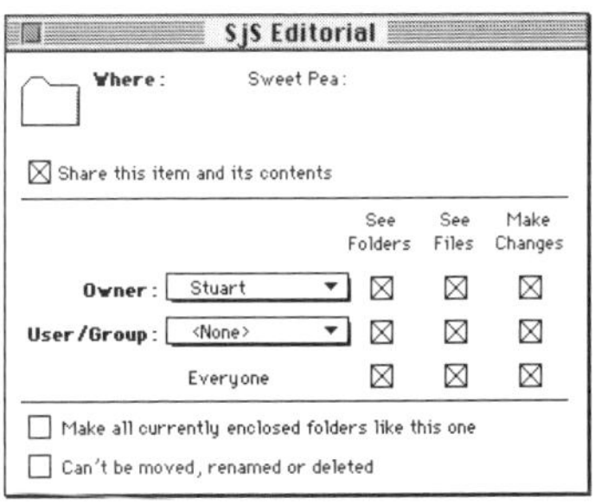

The most important option is the Share this item and its contents check box in the upper-left of the dialog box. This box must be checked before you can use any of the other settings in the dialog box.

Use the first drop-down list to select the Owner for the folder. Unless you are administrating the network or are told to by the person who is the administrator, you should not change the owner or the privileges given to the owner.

The second list lets you assign privileges for a specific user or group. The names of the various users and groups you've created appear in this list. You can specify different access privileges for different users and groups by selecting names from the User/Group drop-down list and then clicking the appropriate check boxes to the right. You define users and groups with the Users & Groups control panel.

The final category, Everyone, controls what privileges are granted to those who connect to your computer but are not a defined user or in a defined group. This includes everyone who connects as a guest to your Mac.

The dialog box for sharing desktop printers is very similar, as you can see from the example shown here.

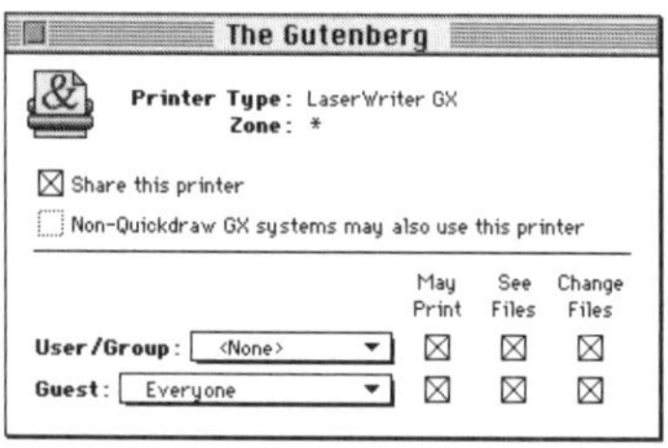

Printers are always owned by the desktop where they are installed, so there isn't a list for Owner. You can use the check box in the upper left to determine whether users who do not have QuickDraw GX installed on their computer may try to use the printer. The options to See Files and Change Files refer to the files that are in the printer's queue waiting to print.

More stuff

Who can use your system is controlled by the Users & Groups control panel. For more on desktop printers, see Part 7.

Mailbox⇨Copy Local

Makes a copy of the selected item on your local hard disk. This command is only available when the actual file for a selected message is located on another machine. You use this command when you want to be sure that you can keep a copy of the file and when you need access to the message even if the other computer is not connected to the network.

Just the facts

Select the message or messages you wish to copy and then choose Mailbox⇨Copy Local. The messages are still stored in your In Tray, but the actual file is now on your computer rather than located somewhere on the network. You can identify messages that are not local by looking at the Location column.

Mailbox⇨In Tray

Opens the window showing all of the messages in your In Tray. This includes any unread messages plus any messages that you have decided to save. To read a message, double-click the message's name. Use Mailbox⇨Out Tray to view your Out Tray, which contains any messages that you have sent but have not been deleted.

Mailbox⇨Mark Read

Marks the selected message or messages as Read. To list only those messages that are marked as Read, choose View⇨Read.

Just the facts

Select the message or messages you wish to change and then choose Mailbox⇨Mark Read. Read messages have a check mark to the left of the message name. Unread message have no mark.

More stuff

TIP

If you have an unread message in your mailbox, every time you open your Key Chain, you are notified that you have new mail. You may want to use Mark Unread on a message that you intend to read later.

REFERENCE

Use Mailbox⇨Unread to remove the check mark that indicates a read message. Use the commands on the View menu to control which messages are displayed.

Mailbox⇨Mark Unread

Marks the selected message or messages as Unread. To list only those messages which are marked Unread, choose View⇨Unread.

Just the facts

Select the message or messages you wish to change and then choose Mailbo⇨Mark Unread. Read messages have a check mark to the left of the message name. Unread messages have no mark.

More stuff

TIP: You should use this command when you've opened a mail message but have not finished reading its contents. The message is marked as read as soon as it's opened, so even if you just glance at the contents of the message, your mailbox marks it as read.

REFERENCE: Use Mailbox⇨Read to mark a message as read without having to open it. Use the commands on the View menu to control which messages are displayed.

Mailbox⇨Out Tray

Displays your Out Tray, which holds any messages that are waiting to be sent or which have not been disposed of. This does not mean that your Out Tray contains a copy of all of the messages you've ever sent. If you wish to keep a record of all the messages that are sent, you need to include yourself on the Recipients list. You can use Mailbox⇨In Tray to switch to viewing the other tray.

Mailbox⇨Preferences

Controls how your mailbox notifies you when a message arrives; controls whether the Special⇨Vistor's Mailbox command is available; controls the order of messages in the mail trays; and controls how long undelivered messages are kept in the Out tray. In addition, you can edit the labels available on the tag list.

Just the facts

As you can see in the following figure, the Mailbox Preferences dialog box is organized into four sections.

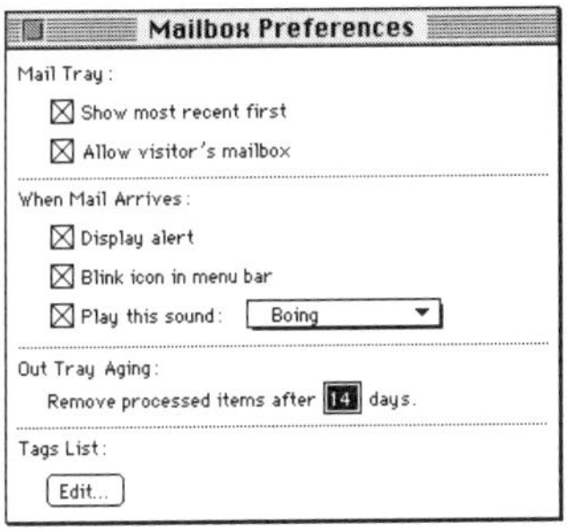

The first section contains two options that control how other commands work. The first option, Show most recent first, controls how messages are displayed within the Mailbox windows and works with the entries on the View menu. When it is checked, message are sorted first by the command on the View menu and then with the most recent first. The second option, Allow vistor's mailbox, must be checked for the Special⇨Vistor's Mailbox command to appear.

The three check boxes in the second section control how you are notified of new mail. You can use any combination of the three, but you should have one of them checked or else you will not be notified. The second option, Blink icon in menu bar, alternates the mailbox icon with the Apple icon at the far left of your menu bar. The icon continues to blink until you open your mailbox. The other two options deliver the notification and then disappear.

The last two sections contain separate features for helping you organize your mail trays. Old messages in the Out Tray are automatically thrown away after the time you indicate. Although a lower number cuts down on the clutter in your Out Tray, a lower number also makes it more likely that an undelivered message will be deleted. The tag list, which you can edit using the final option, is discussed under Mailbox⇨Tag.

More stuff

TIP: To set the total number of letters that are kept in your mailbox, select your mailbox and choose File⇨Get Info. You cannot control how many letters are in each of the two trays separately.

REFERENCE: For information about using tags to group your mail messages, see Mailbox⇨Tag. To find out more about organizing the display of the messages in your trays, see the entries for the commands on the View menu.

Mailbox⇨Send Now

Attempts to deliver the selected message from your Out Tray. That's all there is to this command. You use it when you are viewing your Out Tray (Mailbox⇨Out Tray) to try to force delivery of a message.

Mailbox⇨Tag

Adds or removes a tag from the selected item or items. You should tag your mail messages when you need to be able to sort them into groups. A single item can have multiple tags, and each of the tags represents a separate group.

Just the facts

Select the item or items you wish to tag and then choose Mailbox⇨Tag. You can either select the tag you wish to use from the drop-down list or type the name for the tag. If the name of the tag you enter is not already on the list, it is added. To assign the tag, click the Add button (or press Return). You can add as many tags as you wish to the selected items. When you have added all the tags to the group, click the Done button.

To remove a tag from an item, select the item, choose Mailbox⇨Tag, select the tag you wish to remove, and then click the Remove button. When you are through adding and removing tags, click the Done button.

More stuff

REFERENCE

You can also edit the list of tags by using Mailbox⇨Preferences. To view only the messages with the same tag, use View⇨with Tag.

Network

You use the Network control panel to select which type of network you are using. It also reports the version numbers for all of the network software currently in use. You should not change these settings unless you are installing a new network or experiencing problems with your connection. Even then, it's best if you can convince your local network guru to deal with the problem.

PowerTalk Setup

The most important function served by the PowerTalk control panel is to turn the PowerTalk features on or off. You do that with the check box at the top of the control panel. You can also control the security of your Key Chain by placing a check next to the option to automatically lock the Key Chain after a fixed amount of inactivity. If you always connect your Key Chain when you first start your Mac, you can reduce the steps involved by placing a check next to the Ask for Key Chain Access Code at startup option. In addition, there's a Key Chain button, which is yet another way to access the Apple menu⇨Key Chain command.

Sharing Setup

The most obvious use for the Sharing Setup control panel is to turn on file sharing, but it has several other important uses as well. The Owner Name (usually yourself) is used to create a User account, and all of the folders and disks associated with your Mac are assigned to that user. You can use that user account to access any of the files on your own machine from anywhere on the network (as long as your machine has file sharing turned on). To protect your files, you should always assign a password to the owner's account. (Other accounts are created using the Users & Groups control panel.)

The name you use for your Macintosh appears in everyone else's catalogs across the network. This is the name they will use to send you mail.

The final option in this control panel lets you turn on Program Linking. You should only use this feature if you have a fast machine and other people on the network need to use the programs on your system.

Special⇨I'm at . . .

Stores four sets of mail connections — at home, at work, on the road, and off-line. For each of the first three, you can set which mail services are active, and your Mac remembers your selections. This feature provides a handy way of switching between various configurations of services. Use each of the first three for a different combination of services and simply highlight the option whose settings you want to change. With the off-line option, all of your mail services are disconnected.

Special⇨Lock Key Chain

Locks your Key Chain, which prevents anyone from using your PowerTalk services (such as your mailbox and catalogs) without the Key Chain Access Code (password). If the Key Chain is locked and you try to open your mailbox, you are prompted for the Access Code. You can also unlock the Key Chain by choosing Special⇨Unlock Key Chain (which replaces this command when the Key Chain is locked).

Special⇨Unlock Key Chain

Activates your Key Chain and all of the selected services. When your Key Chain is unlocked, anyone using your Mac can open your mailbox and make changes to your catalogs. After choosing Special⇨Unlock Key Chain, you are prompted for your Access Code (password). After you enter your code and click OK, the command changes to Special⇨Lock Key Chain.

Special⇨Vistor's Mailbox

Creates a mailbox on your desktop for another user. Your normal mailbox is always displayed and your messages always go to your own mailbox. This second mailbox allows someone else who is working on your computer, or in your office, to receive his or her messages. The visitor must have an account on the network and must be able to access the catalog for that account across the network.

Just the facts

After you choose Special⇨Visitor's Mailbox, you are presented with a dialog box that contains a button labeled Choose Catalog and text boxes for a Name and Password. Your own mailbox name will be displayed in the name box. Since you already have a mailbox, you need to replace the name with the visitor's mailbox name and have your visitor enter the password for that mailbox's Key Chain. (It's sorta rude to ask another person for his or her password, so let that person type it in.) You can also use the Choose Catalog button to select your visitor's catalog from across the network, but the password still has to be entered.

Users & Groups

Establish accounts for individuals allowed to use files from your machine across the network. You can also group individual accounts, which makes it possible to give the same access to everyone in the group. You should be very careful about who you let have access to your computer. In many organizations, any changes to the Users & Groups control panel must be approved by your network guru.

Just the facts

When you select the Users & Groups control panel, the first thing you notice is that there are a number of icons for various users and possibly even some for groups. You should see an account for the Owner as identified on the Sharing Setup control panel. The owner's account is identified by its heavier border. You will probably also see an account for a <Guest>. This is the account that is used to decide what privileges an unknown user has when connected to your Mac. A sample Users & Groups control panel with icons for both a New User and a New Group is shown in the following figure. Normally, when you create a new account (either for a user or a group), you immediately change its name.

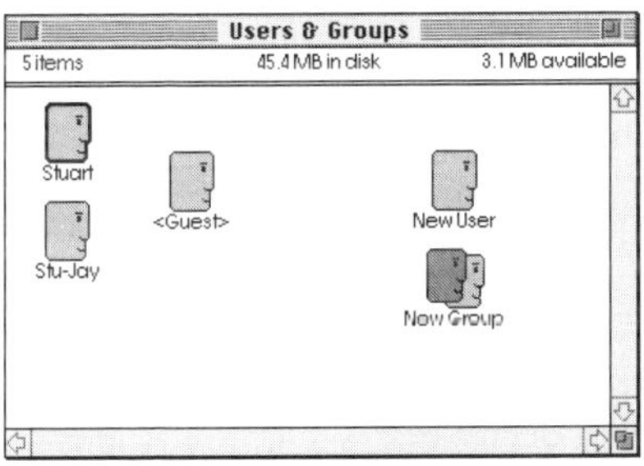

To create a new user account, choose File⇨New User. As soon as the New User icon appears, type the user's account name. To fill in the user's information, double-click the icon for the account. You should always enter a password when you first create an account. You can either ask the person who will own the account to provide a password that you enter, or you can create one yourself and let the person know what it is before using the account.

For the account to be of any use, you have to check the Allow user to connect option. Whether you allow users to change their own passwords is a matter of network policy and personal trust. Because it's a good idea to change passwords frequently, I always prefer to make it the other person's responsibility. Finally, you should only allow program linking if someone else must absolutely use a program that's on your computer. Program Linking will dramatically slow down your system's performance.

To create a new group, choose File⇨New Group. When the New Group icon appears, type the name for the group. To add an individual to the group, drag the icon for that User account onto the group icon. To see the members of the group, double-click the group icon. To remove a member from the group, highlight the name and drag it out of the group window and into the Trash.

To delete a User account entirely, drag it from the Users & Groups control panel into the Trash. That user account is automatically removed from all groups.

More stuff

You use Sharing Setup to actually turn on file sharing and let others connect to your Mac. You use the File⇨Sharing command to control which folders and desktop printers other users may access.

View⇨All

Displays all of the items in a catalog or all of the messages in a mailbox tray. You can use the top portion of the view menu to sort the information, or you can sort the list by clicking one of the column headings. The other commands in the bottom of the View menu, such as View⇨with Tag or View⇨File Servers, are used to restrict the display to certain items or types of messages.

View⇨by Date Sent

Sorts the messages in the tray by the date they were sent. You can sort by one of the other categories by either choosing the appropriate command from the View menu (such as by Location) or by clicking the column heading in the list. Use the bottom part of the View menu to restrict which messages are displayed (View⇨Unread, View⇨Read, or View⇨with Tag). Use View⇨All to display all of the messages in the tray. To display the messages sorted within groups by the time received, use the Show most recent first option after choosing Mailbox⇨Preferences.

View⇨by Kind

Sorts the entries in the catalog by the type of item they represent (their *kind*). Your other option is to sort by Name, which you can do by either choosing the View⇨by Name command or by clicking the Name column heading in the list. You can use View⇨Users, View⇨File Servers, and View⇨Miscellaneous to view only a portion of the catalog; use View⇨All to see all of the entries.

View⇨by Location

Sorts the messages being displayed by the location where they are stored. To sort by another category, either choose it from the View menu (such as View⇨by Priority) or click the column heading (such as Priority) in the list. Use the commands at the bottom of the View menu to control which messages are displayed (View⇨All, View⇨Read, View⇨Unread, and View⇨with Tag). To control the order in which the messages from the same location are displayed, use the Show most recent first option in the Mailbox⇨Preferences dialog box.

View⇨by Name

Sorts the entries in the catalog by the name of each. Your other option is to sort by kind, which sorts based on what type of item each of the entries represents. To sort by kind, either choose the View⇨by Kind command or click the Kind column heading. You can use View⇨Users, View⇨File Servers, and View⇨Miscellaneous to view only a portion of the catalog; use View⇨All to see all of the entries.

View⇨by Priority

Displays the messages in groups based on priority. To display the messages within each group sorted by when they were received, use the Mailbox⇨Preferences command and check the Show most recent first option. To sort by a different category, just click the column heading (such as Sender) or choose the proper command from the View menu (such as View⇨by Sender). You can use the commands at the bottom of the View menu to determine which messages are displayed. Your choices are View⇨All, View⇨Read, View⇨Unread, and View⇨with Tag.

View⇨by Sender

Displays the selected messages in order sorted by the sender. You determine which messages are being displayed by using the commands at the bottom of the View menu (All, Read, Unread, and with Tag). You can sort by a different category by clicking the column heading or by choosing a View menu command. For example, to sort by subject, you can either click the Subject column heading or choose View⇨by Subject. Within groups, you can list the messages with the most recent first by using Mailbox⇨Preferences to set the Show most recent first option.

View⇨by Subject

Organizes the messages in the list so that they are sorted by the subject. If you have more than one message with the same subject, you can use the Mailbox⇨Preferences dialog box to display the most recent first. Use View⇨Read, View⇨Unread, and View⇨with Tag to restrict which messages are displayed; use View⇨All to show all messages in the tray. To change which category you are using to sort the messages, either click the category heading or choose the corresponding command on the View menu (for example, either click the Date Sent column heading or choose View⇨by Date Sent).

View⇨by Unread/Read

Sorts the messages into two groups — those you've marked as read and those marked as unread. With only two groups, you probably should use the Show most recent first option in the Mailbox⇨Preferences dialog box to sort the messages within the groups. You can use Mailbox⇨Mark Read and Mailbox⇨Mark Unread to change which group a message is in. To sort by a different category, either choose the command from the View menu (such as View⇨by Location) or click the column heading. The column on the far left with the check marks is the Read/Unread column. Use View⇨Read, View⇨Unread, and View⇨with Tag to display a smaller group of messages. Use View⇨All to display all of the messages in the tray.

View⇨File Servers

Restricts the list so that it only shows catalogs that contain information about connections to other computers (file servers). To display everything in the catalog, use View⇨All. Use View⇨Users to see just those entries that represent electronic addresses or information cards. You can use View⇨by Kind or View⇨by Name to sort the list.

View⇨Miscellaneous

Displays all of the entries in the list except for those that are for individuals or groups. To display those entries, use either View⇨All (which shows all of the entries) or View⇨Users (which just shows individuals or groups). If you wish to restrict the list further, you can use View⇨File Servers to see only those catalogs that contain information about PowerShare or AppleTalk connections. Sort the list by using either View⇨by Name or View⇨ by Kind.

View⇨Read

Restricts the list to showing only those messages that are marked as read (as indicated with a check mark in the first column). You can sort the list by clicking the column heading for the column you wish to sort by (or by choosing a command from the View menu). To change a message from being read to unread or vice-versa, use Mailbox⇨Mark Read or Mailbox⇨Mark Unread.

View⇨Unread

Only displays those messages which are marked as having not yet been read. You can change whether a message is marked as read by using the Mailbox⇨Mark Read and Mailbox⇨Mark Unread commands. You can change the order in which the messages appear by choosing a command from the top half of the View menu (such as View⇨by Location) or by clicking the column heading you want to sort by (to sort by location, click the Location column heading).

View⇨Users

Shows only those entries that are information cards, electronic addresses, or groups, as well as any catalogs (which might contain information about users). You can sort the information with either the View⇨by Name or View⇨by Kind commands or by clicking the appropriate column heading. To see all of the entries, choose View⇨All. To restrict the view to other categories, use View⇨File Servers or View⇨Miscellaneous.

View⇨with Tag

Displays a dialog box where you can enter the tag that marks those entries you wish to view. Only those entries with that tag are shown in the list. To see all of the entries again, choose View⇨All. To assign a tag to an entry, use Mailbox⇨Tag. You can sort the entries by using any of the commands in the upper portion of the menu (such as View⇨by Sender) or by clicking the column heading for the category that you wish to sort by.

Part 9
Taking It with You: PowerBook Features

Not everybody is chained to a desk all day long. For those with either the freedom to roam or jobs that require a lot of travel, the answer is often a PowerBook — a portable Macintosh. Because the technology required for a portable is different from that used in a desktop machine, System 7.5 has a collection of control panels and other goodies that are only installed on a PowerBook. Well, actually it's truer to say that they're only usable on a PowerBook — they may show up on your desktop Mac by mistake.

If you're using a PowerBook and if everything was installed correctly, you should have a separate PowerBook Guide. It offers information about using those features specific to Apple's line of portable computers. For more information about using the new Apple Guide technology, see the entry for ?⇨Macintosh Guide in Part 2.

Throughout these entries you'll find references to your PowerBook going to sleep and waking up. This doesn't refer to the little men who live inside your computer and flash messages on your screen with flashlights. Instead, *going to sleep* means that your PowerBook has turned off some of the equipment inside to conserve energy. Most often, this means that the screen dims and that the hard disk stops spinning. *Waking up* refers to these pieces of equipment turning back on — the hard disk spins again and information again displays on-screen.

AutoRemounter

One of the most annoying things about using a PowerBook in the office is that whenever it goes to sleep (to save energy), your PowerBook disconnects itself from the network. The AutoRemounter control panel lets you set when your PowerBook will automatically reconnect (only after waking, whenever you turn it on, or never) and whether you need to provide your password when your PowerBook tries to reconnect.

Battery Recondition

On some, but not all, PowerBooks you can use this little program to get additional life out of your battery. It's worth trying, even if you're not sure whether it will work on your system. The worst that will happen is that you will get a notice that this utility won't work with your PowerBook.

Caps Lock

If you've ever had the annoying problem of suddenly typing in all capitals without realizing it because your PowerBook doesn't have a Caps Lock indicator, then this one's for you. When this extension is placed in the Extensions folder within your System Folder, whenever the Caps Lock key is active, a special symbol appears in the menu bar. The special symbol is just a small line with an upward-pointing arrow above it.

Control Strip

NEW 7.5

As control panels go, this one's pretty boring. All it has is an option to choose between Show Control Strip and Hide Control Strip. It's the Control Strip itself that makes it all worthwhile. The Control Strip is an oddly shaped window that appears at the bottom of your PowerBook screen. Why look, here's one now.

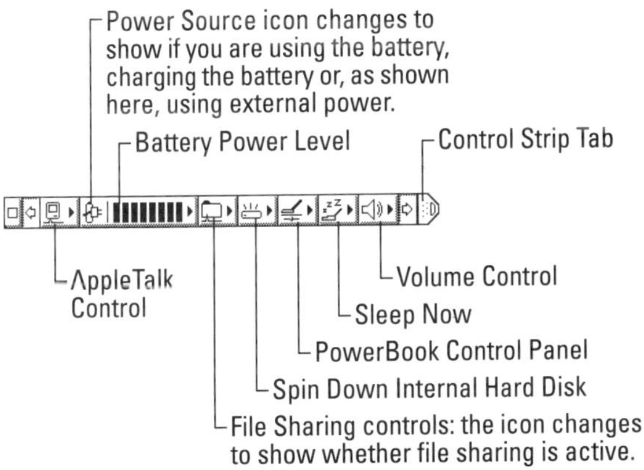

You can double-click the tab at the right of the strip to shrink the Control Strip down to almost nothing (just the tab shows), or you can drag the tab to make the Control Strip any length up to its maximum (where all the modules are showing). When the strip has been reduced so that just the tab shows, double-clicking the tab expands it back to its previous length.

Each of the sections of the Control Strip is a separate utility for managing your PowerBook. These are stored as separate files in the Control Strip Modules folder within your System Folder. You can add a new module to your Control Strip by placing its file within the Control Strip Modules folder. To remove a module, simply remove it from the folder. Of course, it would help if you knew what a module file looked like, so here's a sample.

This module is used to control video mirroring between your PowerBook screen and a larger monitor. This is the same feature that is controlled by the PowerBook Display control panel.

File Assistant

More than a control panel, the File Assistant is a very useful program that actually runs on either a PowerBook or a desktop system. Its primary use, however, is to synchronize the files in two separate folders. *Synchronize,* in this case, means to make sure that both folders contain the same files. This feature is particularly useful if you keep a second copy (called a *backup*) of a folder. To synchronize two folders, open File Assistant (which is probably in a folder named Apple Extras). The File Assistant dialog box, shown in the following figure, appears.

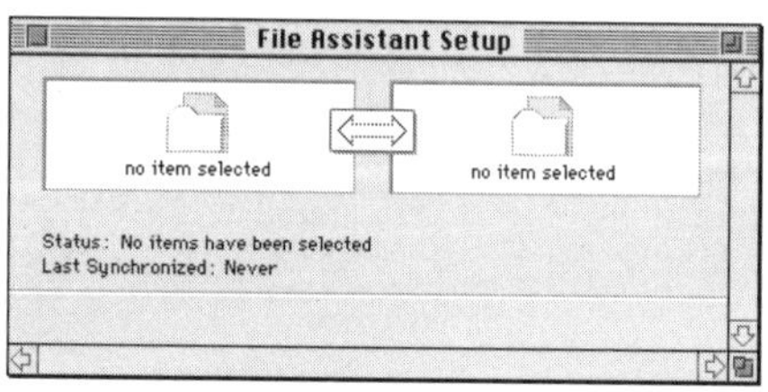

If the folders have different names, you need to choose File➪Preferences and put a check mark next to the Allow non-matching folder names option. (I suggest leaving the other two options checked — they warn you of potential problems.) Close the preference dialog box and then double-click either the left or right half of a pair (where it says *no items selected*). This opens a dialog box where you can select one of the pair of folders that is to be synchronized. After selecting the first in the pair, use the other half to select the second folder. The two folders can be located on the same disk, on different hard disks connected to the same computer, or two disks that are both connected to the network. (You can also synchronize individual files, but that tends to be less useful.)

After you have listed all of your pairs to be synchronized (you can have as many pairs as you wish), you need to decide if both folders are to be updated or whether only changes in one of the folders is reflected in the other. You set this option by choosing the appropriate direction command (Two Way, Left To Right, or Right To Left) from the Synchronize menu. Next, you need to decide whether you want the folders updated automatically or only when you choose the Synchronize⇨Synchronize Now command (or press ⌘-G). If you choose Synchronize⇨Automatic, changes in one folder will be reflected in the other (assuming synchronization is turned on in that direction). To stop having two folders synchronized, select the pair and then choose Edit⇨Delete Pair.

In order for the two folders to be synchronized, your Macintosh must be running File Assistant and both folders must be available to your Mac. You can, however, hide the Setup window by selecting Window⇨Hide Setup Window (or pressing ⌘-H).

For more information about using the File Assistant, choose the ?⇨File Assistant Guide command.

Assistant Toolbox

In order to use the File Assistant, this extension must be placed in the Extensions folder within your System Folder.

PowerBook

The simple story is that the PowerBook control panel can be used to choose between running your PowerBook so that it maximizes performance or so that it conserves the battery and runs longer. If you flip the switch from Easy to Custom, however, you find that there are a variety of other options. To change any of the options independently from the other options, you must turn the Power Conservation to Manual. With it set to Automatic, changing one of the settings changes some or all of the others. You can set the number of minutes of inactivity before the screen dims, before the hard disk spins down, and before the system goes to sleep. In addition, there are options that can increase the amount of time you can use the machine between battery charges — but at the cost of some performance.

PowerBook Display

The PowerBook Display control panel doesn't quite fit in with the rest of the PowerBook entries. That's because there's really a space at the start of its name in the Control Panels folder, so it's one of the first entries. In order to take advantage of this control panel, you need to be using a PowerBook connected to a second monitor. You use the PowerBook Display control panel to switch between having the two monitors display the same information (called *video mirroring*) or function as separate monitors (which requires configuring the Monitors control panel).

PowerBook Setup

Tells programs on your PowerBook whether the modem is external or internal. If you have to plug the modem into the back of your PowerBook, it's external. There's also an option to have your PowerBook wake itself up if it detects an incoming call.

TrackPad

It only makes sense to use this control panel if you have a newer PowerBook with one of the nifty trackpads. This control panel sets how fast you have to push the button in order for your PowerBook to recognize the double-click. You can also set how far you have to move your finger to move the cursor on the screen. If you have a trackball or a mouse attached to your PowerBook, you use the Mouse control panel to configure those devices.

Index

• A •

• B •

• C •

• D •

IDG BOOKS WORLDWIDE REGISTRATION CARD

RETURN THIS REGISTRATION CARD FOR FREE CATALOG

Title of this book: Macintosh System 7.5 For Dummies QR

My overall rating of this book: ❑ Very good [1] ❑ Good [2] ❑ Satisfactory [3] ❑ Fair [4] ❑ Poor [5]

How I first heard about this book:

❑ Found in bookstore; name: [6] ❑ Book review: [7]
❑ Advertisement: [8] ❑ Catalog: [9]
❑ Word of mouth; heard about book from friend, co-worker, etc.: [10] ❑ Other: [11]

What I liked most about this book:

What I would change, add, delete, etc., in future editions of this book:

Other comments:

Number of computer books I purchase in a year: ❑ 1 [12] ❑ 2-5 [13] ❑ 6-10 [14] ❑ More than 10 [15]

I would characterize my computer skills as: ❑ Beginner [16] ❑ Intermediate [17] ❑ Advanced [18] ❑ Professional [19]

I use ❑ DOS [20] ❑ Windows [21] ❑ OS/2 [22] ❑ Unix [23] ❑ Macintosh [24] ❑ Other: [25] ____________ (please specify)

I would be interested in new books on the following subjects:
(please check all that apply, and use the spaces provided to identify specific software)

❑ Word processing: [26] ❑ Spreadsheets: [27]
❑ Data bases: [28] ❑ Desktop publishing: [29]
❑ File Utilities: [30] ❑ Money management: [31]
❑ Networking: [32] ❑ Programming languages: [33]
❑ Other: [34]

I use a PC at (please check all that apply): ❑ home [35] ❑ work [36] ❑ school [37] ❑ other: [38] ____________

The disks I prefer to use are ❑ 5.25 [39] ❑ 3.5 [40] ❑ other: [41] ____________

I have a CD ROM: ❑ yes [42] ❑ no [43]

I plan to buy or upgrade computer hardware this year: ❑ yes [44] ❑ no [45]

I plan to buy or upgrade computer software this year: ❑ yes [46] ❑ no [47]

Name: Business title: [48]

Type of Business: [49]

Address (❑ home [50] ❑ work [51]/Company name:)

Street/Suite#

City [52]/State [53]/Zipcode [54]: Country [55]

❑ **I liked this book!**
You may quote me by name in future IDG Books Worldwide promotional materials.

My daytime phone number is ____________

IDG BOOKS

THE WORLD OF COMPUTER KNOWLEDGE